Scotch Whisky
ITS PAST and PRESENT

David Daiches grew up in Edinburgh, where he attended George Watson's College and Edinburgh University before proceeding to Balliol College, Oxford, where he was a Bradley Fellow. He subsequently taught at universities on both sides of the Atlantic (including Chicago, Cornell, Cambridge and Sussex). His last academic post was as Director of the Institute for Advanced Studies in the Humanities at Edinburgh. He has published some forty-five books of literary criticism, history and biography, and holds honorary degrees from universities in Scotland, England, France, Italy, the USA and Canada. In 1991 he was awarded the CBE for services to literature.

SCOTCH WHISKY
ITS PAST AND PRESENT

DAVID DAICHES

Birlinn

This edition published 1995 by
Birlinn Limited
13 Roseneath Street
Edinburgh EH9 1JH

First published by Andre Deutsch Ltd 1969

ISBN 1 874744 36 X

A CIP record of this book is available
from the British Library

Detail from portrait of *Indulging*
by William Kidd by kind permission of
The National Gallery of Scotland

Designed by Gourlay Graphics Glasgow

Made and printed in Finland by
Werner Söderström OY

Contents

Preface

This book does not claim to be a complete and authoritative account of all aspects of Scotch whisky. My concern has been with its social history, its nature, and its present situation. Where matters of taste are concerned, my view is, of course, a personal one, but with respect to matters of fact I have tried to be accurate and objective. I have been helped in this latter endeavour by the kindness and co-operation of people concerned with Scotch whisky at all levels. Firms have sent me their house histories, directors have given up time to talk to me at length, distillery managers have patiently answered my questions and interrupted their work to entertain as well as inform me, brewers, maltmen and stillmen have tolerated with great courtesy my butting in on their routine activities to observe and question. My son has been given every possible facility for taking photographs both in distilleries and in blending and bottling plants. It is true that when I was rash enough to ask one of the great blending firms if they could let me know the proportion of malt and grain whisky in each of the two blends they put out I received a letter informing me that 'it is with regret that I have to tell you that this information is "classified", and that therefore we will not be able to help you with this section of your book'. But on all other matters everybody has been most forthcoming, and my son and I have received nothing but kindness. I have to thank Messrs. Harpers, publishers of *Harpers Wine and Spirit Gazette*, for permission to reproduce their map of the Scotch whisky distilleries.

My expression of gratitude for so much friendly assistance must not, however, obscure the central fact that the opinions expressed in this book are my own. I know that my views on some points are not shared by some of those who have helped me with information, but even when they are shared

I must emphasize that nobody but myself is responsible for the views enunciated in various parts of the book. In some respects this is a very personal account of Scotch whisky, for after all the enjoyment of Scotch whisky is a very personal activity. But I have tried to get the facts right.

It is often maintained by those in the Scotch whisky trade that the future of their product depends on the continued expansion of exports. From the point of view of those consumers who most enjoy it, however, it might be said with equal truth that the spread of knowledge and discrimination with respect to it is the best guarantee of its future. Scotch whisky is known throughout the world as a drink of great character and individuality. One purpose of this book is to help increase awareness of that character and individuality so as to preserve and indeed enhance the reputation of Scotch whisky not simply as an alcoholic stimulant but as a civilized drink of great range and subtlety that is best consumed with attention and judgement.

David Daiches

Preface to 1995 Edition

In the quarter-century since this book first appeared the Scotch whisky trade has seen many changes. In the original edition I traced the early years of Scotch whisky and charted the changes brought about in the nineteenth century by the invention of the patent still and the development of blended grain and malt whisky, emphasising the significant part played by the Distillers Company Limited. The movement from a cottage industry to family firms to great international companies has proceeded further in the last twenty-five years. DCL itself, which played such an important part in the development of blended Scotch whisky as a world drink, has now become United Distillers, and the internationalising of the Scotch whisky trade has proceeded much further. Japanese, Canadian, American and French firms have now significant interests in Scottish distilleries and the Scotch whisky trade is now firmly in the world of multi-national companies. The complex relationships between distillers, blenders, brokers, exporters, merchants and international finance houses is now far beyond the reach of the combination of cultural historian and discriminating taster that I considered myself to be when I wrote this book.

Nevertheless, in spite of the dizzy developments of the last decade, the nature and quality of Scotch whisky remains unchanged. Though some classic distilleries have been closed, others have re-opened and some new ones have been built. Most significant of all, the knowledge and appreciation of single malt whiskies – varieties of the true original post-still Highland malt whisky – has grown enormously and continues to grow. One can now get great malt whiskies at wine merchants and pubs throughout Britain and in bars and shops on the Continent and throughout the U.S.A. While blended whisky continues to represent the bulk of the Scotch whisky sold throughout the world, the great single malts flourish as they have never flourished before, often sponsored by clubs and societies dedicated to their discriminating enjoyment.

The account of the origins and development of Scotch whisky, of its social history and of the products of different distilleries, can stand unchanged as a necessary background to the understanding of recent developments. The reader will appreciate what a long way whisky has come throughout the centuries, and realise at the same time how many essential matters, notably the quality of the drink itself, remain unchanged. Whatever has happened in the complex world of international buying and selling, the taste, nose and individuality of the product of a Scotch whisky distillery remains unique and remarkable.

David Daiches,
Edinburgh, November 1994

The Origins and Nature of Scotch Whisky

A rugged country with a stormy history : Scotland, with its mountains and glens and lochs and streams, captures the visitor with its beauty and its legends, and haunts the exile with insistent memories. The Highlands are the most striking part, with their physical grandeur and their picturesque and sometimes terrible past of clan loyalty and clan warfare. But Scotland has its fertile fields and its great cities as well as its mountain glory, while the Border country, with a scenic display less spectacular but no less appealing than the Highlands, has its own romantic story that finds expression in the great Border Ballads. The popular view of Scotland is understandably somewhat starry-eyed – or perhaps misty-eyed would be the better term : Loch Lomond, the Hebrides, heather-clad hills, and St Andrews, the silver city by the sea where the royal and ancient game of golf first became an institution. But Scotland has another side too : it was in Glasgow and on Clydeside that the Industrial Revolution began, and that corner of the country is still one of the great industrial areas of the world. And Edinburgh, the capital, with its Castle and its ring of hills, its narrow and history-soaked Old Town and its spacious and elegant New Town, one of the half-dozen most beautiful cities in the world; Aberdeen, the Granite City in the northeast, fronting the cold North Sea with courage and dignity; Inverness, the capital of the Highlands; Perth, the ancient royal burgh looking equally to the Highland north and the Lowland south, scene of the most terrible of all clan battles in the late fourteenth century – each of these has its own atmosphere, its own story to tell. Add to all this the wearing o' the kilt and the gay appeal of tartan, the haunting quality of bagpipe music, and the nostalgia for a lost independence which is still active in the Scottish imagination, and you get a picture that can hardly fail in its box-office appeal.

Yet Scotland, contrary to what one might sometimes be led to think, is neither a stage backcloth nor a film script, but a real country with real problems. And its best known product, Scotch whisky, is not a whimsical mountain dew distilled by pixies but a spirit produced by human art and sold in vast quantities all over the world. It was not always, of course, an internationally known drink, as the pages that follow will make clear. For centuries its production and consumption was largely confined to the Highlands. For it is the Gaelic-speaking Highland clans whom we have to thank for this contribution to the joy of living. The word 'whisky' itself derives from the Gaelic *uisge beatha*, 'water of life'.

When and how the Highlanders first produced whisky we do not know. Neil Gunn, the Scottish novelist and whisky expert, has a charming fantasy of the accidental distillation of steam rising from ground and fermented barley as it boiled in a pot under the eye of some primitive clansman who proceeded at once to experiment with its consumption and to inform his friends; Gunn goes on to tell how the band of secret drinkers were surprised by the Elders, who themselves experimented with the liquor, so that knowledge of it then came to the Druid and the Chief. Gunn does not say whether his primeval discoverer of whisky was a Pict (early inhabitant of Scotland who occupied the extreme north and north-east) or a Scot. The Scots came from Ireland in the fifth century AD, bringing to Scotland their Gaelic language and the name eventually to be adopted by the country as a whole. Was it the Scots who brought the art of distilling with them from Ireland? Douglas Young, the Scottish poet and scholar, used to maintain that whisky was invented by the Irish as an embrocation for sick mules and that once it was brought to Scotland its use was perverted from external animal application to internal human consumption. But Young was not a whisky drinker and his account is clearly an amusing invention. Nevertheless, there is reason to believe that the art of distilling whisky was developed very early in Ireland. An Irish legend says that Saint Patrick first taught the art, but it makes no mention of sick mules, so that presumably the saint intended it for human drinking. A German historian of distilling says that at one time old Irish Celtic ruins near Cashel were believed to contain the remains of bronze distilling apparatus. When Henry II of England invaded Ireland in 1172 he is said to have found the distillation of spirits from grain well established there. And since we use the term 'whisky' to denote a spirit distilled from grain as distinct from a spirit distilled from grapes or other sorts of fruit or berries, this would suggest that the Irish were drinking a form of whisky in the twelfth century.

Perhaps, then, distilling was brought from Ireland to Scotland some time in the early Middle Ages, but we cannot be certain. A second German authority on distilling has roundly denounced the story of the origin of distilling in Ireland, and in particular of Saint Patrick's invention of it, as wholly unhistorical. All we know is that Irish whiskey (traditionally and still today distilled from a mash of un-malted barley and other grains) and Scotch whisky (distilled from malted barley only) have a history of many centuries. The first recorded allusion to a spirit distilled from barley in Scotland is found in the Scottish Exchequer Rolls for 1494, which notes the provision of 'eight bolls of malt to Friar John Cor wherewith to make aquavitae'. (*Aqua vitae*, 'water of life', is the traditional name for a distilled spirit : it is the exact Latin equivalent of the Gaelic *uisge beatha* and the French *eau de vie*.) But, of course, before a process of this kind surfaces into recorded history it is likely to have had a long run. The whole early history of distilling is still a debating ground for scholarly argument and conjecture. It seems to have been known in the Far East at a very early date. Arab chemists inherited the traditions of the Alexandrian chemists of the first nine hundred years AD and developed a variety of modes of distilling, though not with a view to producing potable spirits. The word 'alcohol' comes to us from the Arabic. Medieval alchemists learned something from the Arabs, and the great thirteenth-century philosopher and theologian Albertus Magnus wrote an account of how to produce by distillation what he called

aqua ardens, 'burning water'. The thirteenth-century
Spanish philosopher and alchemist Raymond Lull also
studied and wrote about distilling. The distillation of wine
into brandy in France was known in the thirteenth century
and developed as a manufacturing industry in the fourteenth. It was also in the Middle Ages that the production
of perfumes and extracts of herbs and flowers for medicinal
use first developed, a process involving distillation. A variety
of spirits for drinking, made both from grapes and from
grain, developed throughout Europe, first as medicine and
then as a drink to be consumed for pleasure : first liqueurs,
made of alcohol, sugar or syrup, and flavouring matter;
then brandy from France; then grain spirits whose origins
we have just been puzzling over. And, as we have seen,
Scotch whisky was well established in Scotland by the end
of the fifteenth century.

But why Scotland and why Scotch whisky? What is so
special about Scotland that it should have produced a
unique spirit now known all over the world? Of course,
one could point to the range of mean temperatures in Scotland and argue that any country that is liable to stay pretty
chilly the whole year round requires the regular imbibing
of an agreeable spirituous drink. In Scotland it does not get
cold enough in the winter to encourage the periodic consumption of vast quantities of crude alcoholic spirit in order
to forget the cold and the dark, such as one still sometimes
finds in the more northerly parts of Scandinavian countries.
The Scottish climate is never numbing, and if you walk
across the heather with a fine drizzle coming down and the
temperature about 55° Fahrenheit you will find everything
round you enchantingly *fragrant.* The Scottish countryside
always smells nice, whether you crush the leaves of the bog
myrtle as you tramp the hillsides and inhale its lovely
characteristic odour or simply receive in a more general
way the varied smells of bush and flower and grass and
peat and (one would be prepared to swear) of the air and
the water themselves. The countryside is never dried up in
Scotland; it is always damp, alive, fragrant. It is no surprise,
therefore, that the traditional Scottish drink makes its

primary appeal to the nose. With the climate cold enough for the national drink to have to be a warming one but not so cold as to drive people to any alcoholic expedient in order to find inner warmth or even oblivion, and with the countryside making continuously olfactory demands on the inhabitants, Scotland, one could argue, was bound to produce a spirit of rare and subtle aroma. Further, Scotland is too far north to allow the massive growing of grapes, but it has for many centuries produced barley, that most hardy of all cereal grains, so that a barley spirit ('barley bree' in the old Scots phrase) rather than a grape spirit would be the natural one. Then, again, the Highlands of Scotland teem with the most beautiful clear water from stream and spring, and there are many peat bogs; so that if you need peat smoke in order to dry the barley and turn it into aromatic malt, and clear water for the further process of turning that malt into a fermented liquid before distilling it into spirit, there too Nature has laid everything on your doorstep.

What, then, *is* Scotch whisky? What is it made of, and how? These questions are not as simple as may be supposed, as a later chapter will show : a distinguished King's Counsel assisted by a bench of lay magistrates tried in vain to decide what whisky was in a famous case in 1906, and as a result of their inability a Royal Commission was set up in 1907 to settle the unresolved question, with fateful consequences for the future of Scotch whisky. But before looking at the problems created by later inventions and practices, let us consider what Scotch whisky originally, authentically and uniquely was and is. What is the distinctive spirit that only Scotland has been able to produce (in spite of honest efforts to produce it elsewhere out of the same ingredients by exactly the same process)? There are, of course, other kinds of whisky, some admirable in their own way, produced in other countries. But the whisky distilled from malted barley in the manner perfected in the Scottish Highlands in the eighteenth century and still produced in essentially the same manner – what we call Pot Still Highland Malt Scotch Whisky – has proved to be inimitable outside Scotland.

Scotch Whisky

I have tasted a blended Scotch whisky produced in Canada from imported Highland malt whisky and locally produced grain whisky which was quite a respectable drink; but the true malt whiskies of Scotland remain a Scottish 'mystery' in both senses of that word. I have been told by a friend who was in the Far East during the last war that he came across a bottle labelled 'King Victoria Finest Scotchman's Whisko' allegedly made in Japan (where quantities of less eccentrically labelled whisky are certainly made and drunk today, some of it a blend of imported Scottish malt whisky and local spirit). There have been many attempts, both scrupulous and unscrupulous, to break Scotland's monopoly of Scotch. But the monopoly remains.

Barley, water and peat are what is needed to produce the malt whisky of Scotland. Though barley is not Scotland's main cereal crop, which for centuries has been oats, it is still a significant and traditional crop in Scotland. In the great whisky-producing area of Scotland, a vast rectangle immediately south of the Moray Firth in the north-east of the country, there is a coastal plain as well as valleys where barley has long been grown and where originally the distillers obtained all their barley. The combination of cold, clear streams tumbling rapidly down mountain sides with fertile valleys, of wild Highland scenery with a rich and gentle coastal plain, is characteristic of this part of Scotland. The local availability of barley, water and peat made the distilling of whisky a natural part of the rhythm of life and work, bound up with the economy of the Scottish countryside. Distilling was carried on between October and May, although today many distilleries work throughout the year, except for a few weeks in summer, used for annual holidays and necessary building or maintenance. The by-products of the process were available for use as cattle-feed during the winter months; in the summer, when there was no need of artificial cattle-feed, distillation was suspended and the distilleries cleaned and overhauled. It must be emphasized that traditionally the distilling of Scotch whisky took its place, as to a large extent it still does, as part of the normal routine of a farming community.

Barley, then, is where the process begins. Though few of us may have seen

> reapers, reaping early
> In among the bearded barley

most of us will have seen fields of barley with the characteristic 'bearded' tops glinting pale in the sun. Some of us may have examined more closely an ear of barley with its two longitudinal rows of grain (in the case of the common 'two-rowed' barley) and the spiky beard extending well beyond. The barley bought by the distiller is, of course, in grain form : he fills his lofts with great piles of ripe grain, each grain with its pale, wrinkled skin, shuttle-shaped and with a sweetish smell. Although originally it was always local barley that was used, some of the greatest Highland malt Scotch whiskies today use imported barley. This has been going on for some time, and it is clear that the quality of the whisky does not depend on its being made from home-grown barley. The water and the peat, however, do demonstrably contribute in large measure to the quality of the whisky, though the peat is not always local; some Highland malt distillers get their malt ready-made from Pitsligo, Aberdeenshire, or Kirkcaldy, Fife, and an increasing number have given up doing their own malting. Different distilleries produce whiskies of different 'nose', body and flavour in the same way as different French vineyards, producing wine from the same variety of grape by the same process, produce quite different vintages; and this clearly has something to do with the peat and the water. There are many other factors, some quite intangible and very difficult to put one's finger on, which account both for the uniqueness of Scottish[1] pot-still malt whisky and for the differences between pot-still malt whiskies made by different distilleries in different parts of the country. A look at the actual processes involved may help to explain this.

While it is true that some of the finest Scotch whisky has for a long time been made with imported barley, it does not follow that the quality of the barley does not matter. It matters very much. The first process in making the whisky is *malting*, the turning of barley into malt. To do this properly, and to produce malt of the desired quality, the barley must be fully ripened, plump, thoroughly sound, dry and of the proper protein content. If the barley is not sufficiently dry it will go mouldy during storage. (As the barley is usually all bought at the same time of the year, in September or October during or just after the harvest, enough must be bought to provide for the year's malting, so storage is important.) Mouldy barley will not germinate properly, and germination is an essential process in malting. So after the barley has been carefully screened from impurities it is dried either on kilns in batches or in storage towers in a continuous process involving the passing of warm air over the grain.[2] The properly dry barley is stored in large bins until needed for malting.

Malt is essentially barley that has been allowed to germinate by soaking in water and has then been dried by the application of heat. Because of its high carbohydrate and protein content, malt has long been regarded as a body builder for growing children and prescribed for what used to be called 'wasting diseases'. When I was a child, I used to be dosed with 'extract of malt with cod-liver oil' every morning after breakfast. But the part played by malt in brewing and distilling has nothing to do with its status as a symbol of strength. Unlike unmalted barley, malt when ground and mashed with water converts its starch into a mixture of soluble compounds including the crystalline sugar known as maltose and by doing so makes fermentation possible. Fermentation produces a beer-like liquid and is the first stage in distilling. (Brewing is thus a process common to the making of beer, where it is the end process, and the production of whisky, where it is an intermediate process. This intermediate fermenting or brewing process in a distillery is under the supervision of the brewer, who is the most highly paid workman in any distillery.)

The first step in the malting process is to soak the barley in tanks or 'steeps' to promote germination. The period of the soaking varies according to weather conditions, the time of the year and the grade of barley; it can be as little as forty-eight hours and as much as seventy. An experienced maltster can tell whether the barley has been soaked long enough by pressing it between his thumb and forefinger, but modern distilleries also provide laboratory tests of the moisture content.[8]

After the barley has been soaked for the requisite amount of time, the water is drained off and the grain is spread out to a depth of two or three feet on a stone, concrete or tiled floor in the malting house. Here the sweet dusty smell which assails the nostrils when one visits the original barley store has given way to a distinctive smell which though not unpleasant I can best describe as a warm mouldiness. It is here on the malting floor that the germination develops, a process during which the barley 'breathes' – taking in oxygen and expiring carbon dioxide – and generates a considerable amount of heat. In order to control the rising temperature (which is highest at the bottom) the grain is regularly turned by maltmen with wooden shovels or 'skips' : this process also prevents growing rootlets from becoming entangled with each other and producing a matted mess. The 'turning' of the 'piece' – to express it in technical malting language – is a somewhat stylized operation, involving tossing the grain into the air with a rhythmic movement of the skip; but I have never heard of any traditional worksongs associated with this activity. The maltmen work in silence. As a result of the daily or more often twice-daily turning, the barley is thinned out in a period of from eight to fourteen days to a level of a few inches. By this time the 'acrospire' or growing stem of the barley has grown to five-eighths of the length of the seed. Further growth must be stopped and this is done by further turning and thinning, as well, sometimes, as 'ploughing', the actual dragging by hand of a plough through the grain. During the whole process the head maltman has been careful to maintain the temperature of the germinating grain at about 60° F. Turning the barley in the traditional way on the malting floor is an arduous business, and some distilleries now use more labour-saving methods. Sometimes huge revolving drums are used (each holding from ten to fifty tons of barley) with cool air blown through a central inlet to control the heat produced by the germinating grain. Some distilleries use the long concrete or metal trench known as the 'Saladin box' after Charles Saladin, the French engineer who invented it. In the Saladin box revolving metal forks move slowly up and down its length to keep the grain turned and aerated.

Whether done on the traditional malting floor, or in large drums, or in Saladin boxes, the germination process is now as complete as is required and further growth is stopped. The grains are now soft and chalky. 'When you can write your name on the wall with it,' an old maltman once told Neil Gunn, 'it's ready.' The barley has been turned into 'green malt' and is ready for the drying kiln. The starch in the grain can now be converted into fermentable sugar.[4]

Green malt is not literally green – in fact it looks very like the original malted barley grains, a pale straw colour. It contains a considerable amount of moisture, and is transferred to the kiln for drying. It is the kiln that has the 'pagoda head' which proclaims the distillery on the landscape. The floor of the kiln is of perforated iron or wire mesh. Here the green malt is spread at a depth of between one and three feet (depending on the design of the kiln) and dried in the smoke arising from a peat fire some ten or fifteen feet below. The open ventilator at the top – which is the pagoda head – draws up the hot air from the fire through the green malt on the perforated floor. The peat is of the first importance as it gives its special flavour to the malt and eventually to the mature whisky. The smell of burning peat is an agreeable domestic smell when one experiences it in front of a peat fire in a Highland cottage. But if you put your face into the kiln when the peat smoke ('peat reek' as the Scots say) is billowing you will soon feel that enough is enough. The smoke stings the eyes and catches you in the throat, and though you may recognize that this is the flavour which will one day marvellously enrich the taste and bouquet of the matured whisky, you

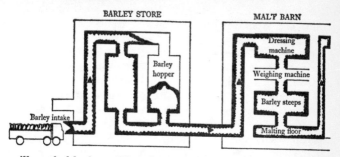

will probably be willing to wait for your next encounter until you meet it in the glass.

In the old days, peat was the sole fuel used, but now coke or anthracite is often also used to provide heat, and peat used only to provide flavour. The drying begins in peat smoke, but after about twenty-four hours coke or anthracite is substituted and the temperature – which has been carefully regulated from the beginning, rising slowly over the peat fire – is raised further until the malt has been dried to the point of retaining only about 3 per cent of its moisture.

The traditional method of kiln drying has given way in some modern distilleries to a more rapid method of achieving the same result. Instead of using the principle of natural draught, with a ventilator at the top drawing up the hot air, these modern kilns have fans for blowing in warm, peat-flavoured air, so that the malt is dried quickly under pressure. Several distilleries now buy all or a part of their malt ready-made (and peated to the desired degree) from specialist malt producers outside their own region.

The malt is now ready – dry, crisp, friable, aromatic, very different in texture and flavour from the original barley though scarcely distinguishable in appearance. It is stored in bins to await the time when it is needed for the next processes – mashing and brewing. But before it goes on to mashing it is cleansed of the 'combings' or rootlets and any other impurities by being passed through a dressing machine. The combings used to be sold as cattle food under the name of 'malt culms'. It is then coarsely ground in a mill. The ground malt (malt grist) then goes into the *mash tun*, which is a large circular vat of several thousand gallons' capacity. It is released into the mash tun from a hopper in carefully measured quantities (indeed, there is a great deal of weighing and measuring in the whole process of whisky production, since at each point a given quantity of raw material is expected to produce a given quantity of the product at the next stage) together with hot water. This mashing with hot water helps to complete the conversion of dextrin into maltose. The malt is extracted three and sometimes four times with hot water, each time at a different temperature, ranging from about 160° F. for the first to over 180° F. for the last. The resulting liquid is called *wort* (pronounced 'wurt') or *worts*. (I have heard the plural form more often than the singular in distilleries.) The wort produced by the first two washings is drained out through the bottom of the tun into the *underback* or worts receiver; the product of the later washings (*sparge*) becomes the first and second extractions of the next batch. The solids that remain after the wort is run off are known as *draff*, which (like malt culms) is used as a winter cattle food. Mashing, by the way, is a smelly process : the characteristic smell that hangs around a distillery is compounded of many factors, but the pungent smell of the mashing is central.

The thick porridge-like substance which was produced by the ground malt and hot water, when the mashing process started, was very different from the wort we now have : this is a sweet (and oddly sweet-smelling) semi-transparent liquid, not yet alcoholic. Sir Robert Bruce Lockhart recalled how as a boy on holiday at his maternal grandfather's distillery of Balmenach he 'was often allowed to taste this sugary water and found it pleasant' : but I have heard of no other case of wort being used as a child's soft drink.

From the underback the wort is run into a refrigerator, because unless it is cooled (to about 70° F.) the maltose would decompose and the yeast used in the next process, brewing, would be killed by the heat. From the refrigerator it is run into the *wash-back*, a huge vat holding up to

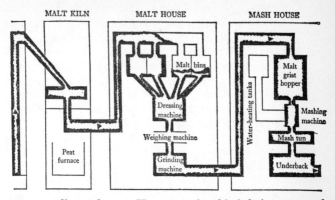

10,000 gallons of wort. Here yeast is added, being pumped in simultaneously with the wort, and as a result fermentation takes place. (A distillery of any size will have several wash-backs – a large one will have eight or ten.) The enzymes of the yeast then do their duty, first producing dextrose from the maltose and then converting the dextrose into alcohol and carbon dioxide.[5] It is a violent and noisy process. At first there is just the rising of faintly plopping bubbles, but gradually the activity in the liquid increases. The production of carbon dioxide causes it to froth and seethe and the brewer in charge has the responsible task of keeping it under control and seeing that it does not boil over. The wash-backs are never filled to the top, but three or four feet of space is left between the surface of the liquid and the top of the wash-back to allow for the bubbling and boiling. Even so, constant care is needed. Formerly, men with sticks of birch-wood would control the threatening liquid by beating, but for a long time now this has been done by mechanical stirrers. At the end of the process, which takes anything from thirty-six to forty hours, we have a clear liquid, known simply as the *wash*, which consists of water, yeast and a bit over 5 per cent by volume of alcohol (i.e. about 10° proof). Thus the wash, like beer, is a liquid that has been brewed but not distilled.[6]

The next process, distillation, is what actually produces

the whisky. What is involved in distilling is essentially turning a liquid into vapour and then condensing the vapour back into liquid. If you hold a cold knife over the steam that comes from a boiling kettle, drops of water will condense on to the knife. If you heat wash in a copper pot and then condense the vapour that rises from the boiling wash by passing it in a pipe through a tub of cold water, you are going through the basic process of making whisky. Scotch whisky is a distillation of a fermented brew which has in turn been made by the addition of yeast to ground malt extracted with hot water. Though the modern method I am now describing incorporates a number of improvements, and involves operation on a larger scale, the process is essentially the same as that used in the eighteenth century and very probably much earlier than that. Highland malt Scotch whisky was and is distilled in pear-shaped copper stills ('pot stills'). Every distillery must have at least two such stills, the wash still (often with a somewhat larger neck) in which the wash is first distilled to produce 'low wines', and the low wines still in which the impure dilute spirit of the low wines is distilled a second time, this time to produce whisky. Though the two stills may differ slightly in shape, each is of the same general design, bulbous at the bottom, narrow at the top, with a narrow neck extending downwards through the wall of the still house to the coiled copper pipe – the *worm* – which lies in a tank of cold water. This, then, is the simple and ancient process of distilling : the liquid is heated until it vaporizes; the vapour passes up the neck of the still and down through the worm where the lower temperature produced by the surrounding cold water causes it to condense into liquid again. The distillate from the wash goes first into the spirit safe and then into the low wines charger whence it goes to be redistilled in the low wines still. The low wines distillate is also run into the spirit safe, where it is tested until the initial highly impure samples (*foreshots*) have given way to true whisky, at which point it is run into the spirit receiver. The last part of the distillate is, like the first part, impure : this is known as *feints* and is turned into a feints receiver to be redistilled

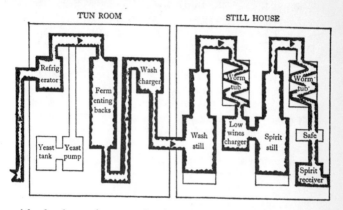

with the low wines – and with the foreshots – in the next batch.

There is no universally accepted way of heating the pot stills. Many are heated by coal fires, some by oil-fired furnaces. Some of the most recent distilleries heat by steam coils inside the still (Glenmorangie has been doing this since the 1880s). But coal furnaces with automatic stokers seem to be as far towards modernization as many Highland malt distilleries are willing to go. Some distillers insist that coal is the best fuel; the pockets of hot flaring gas – 'hot points' or 'flash points' – which a coal fire produces, they maintain, assist the rise of the vapour in the still.

It is the responsibility of the stillman to test the samples so as to determine when the low wines still is producing acceptable whisky. The clear foreshot turns cloudy when water is added; when it ceases to turn cloudy with the addition of water, it is true whisky. Yet a stillman may not be satisfied with this test. I remember once watching a stillman at work at Laphroaig distillery and thinking that the tests showed that the whisky was ready. 'Not yet,' said the stillman, eyeing the sample closely, 'it's still a bit *blue*.' So we waited a further five minutes, by which time the faint blueness had gone and the distillate could be run into the spirit receiver.

The spirit safe through which the distillate is passed is rather like a large brass box or trunk with glass sides. It is constructed so that by turning the appropriate tap the stillman can pass the spirit into a vessel fitted with a hydrometer for measuring the specific gravity, or dilute it with a given proportion of distilled water. (It is important that these operations be done under glass, with the spirit not available for actual tasting, since the excise officer is responsible for checking and safeguarding the quantity of spirit that is produced.) A handle on the outside of the safe can deflect the acceptable whisky to the spirit receiver. What is unacceptable – foreshots and feints – is run into the low wines and feints receiver for redistilling.

The precise moment at which the distillate is turned into the spirit receiver depends on the stillman's judgement, as does the moment towards the end of the process when the distillate is becoming feints and must be deflected from the spirit receiver. There are no hard and fast rules, nor is there an absolutely 'pure' whisky produced in the middle period of distilling which can be clearly distinguished from fore-shots at the beginning and feints at the end. The aldehydes, esters, furfurol and other compounds of hydrogen, oxygen and carbon formed in the process of distilling the wash and known generally as *congenerics* are present in excess in the foreshots but they also give pot-still malt whisky its special bouquet and flavour, so it is not a question of eliminating them, but of nice judgement, based on long experience, of exactly when to regard the whisky as a true potable spirit and when to stop so regarding it. The making of whisky is an art, and at every stage the objective knowledge provided by the scientist must be supplemented (as historically it was anticipated) by an almost intuitive skill produced by years of practice and often by a long family tradition, for distillery workers tend to run in families. A mistake – running the foreshots into the spirit receiver by deflecting the distillate into it too soon, or waiting too long before turning the distillate away from the spirit receiver – may not be immediately noticed, but could have disastrous consequences for the flavour of the whisky many years later, when it is fully matured and all the potentialities of its bouquet and flavour are realized.

The residue of the wash, still known as *burnt ale* or *pot ale*, is removed – it is sometimes turned into fertilizer or, evaporated and dried, into animal food – and the still is thoroughly cleaned before the next distillation. The residue of the low wines still, *spent lees*, is little more than water, with sometimes very small amounts of copper from the still in solution : it is of no use or value and is simply run off. There is a problem of water pollution in running away the burnt ale, serious in view of the importance of trout and salmon fishing in Scottish streams and rivers. Some distilleries have their own plant for converting pot ale and draff into animal feeding stuff or fertilizer. Glenlivet distillery has joined with the Chivas distilleries in building an effluent plant to produce 'dark grains'. Effluent from Mortlach and three other distilleries is now processed in a plant at Convalmore Distillery, between Dufftown and Craigellachie. Scottish Malt Distillers Ltd. (see page 111) has built six effluent processing plants. The biggest such plant in the country is the Combination of Rothes Distillers Dark Grains Plant, where twelve distillers co-operate in running a plant which re-cycles their waste products : it weekly converts 1·3 million gallons of pot ale and 1700 tons of wet draff into 600 tons of 'dark grains'. The 'dark grains', in pellet form, are sold for mixing with other substances to form nutritious cattle food.

Distilleries are not, as a rule, especially beautiful buildings, though some are beautifully situated and some are maintained with a sharper eye to outward appearance than others (Laphroaig, for example, with its sparkling white-wash and gay window-boxes, not for nothing the only distillery run by a woman). Nor is the lay-out always the most rational. The movement from barley store to malting floor to malt kiln to malt bins to grinding mill to grist hopper to mash tun to wash-backs to wash still to low wines still to spirit receiver would, one might imagine, normally be planned in a continuous flow in as near a straight line as possible. But in many of the older distilleries there is doubling back and a good deal of twisting and turning to accommodate everything needed in the available space. Newer distilleries, such as Tormore, are rationally planned with a lay-out which minimizes unnecessary movement.

The shape and size of the pot still affect the quality of the whisky produced. I have heard a stillman maintain that the higher the still the better, as the fewer impurities emerge in the distillate, and certainly the form of the top does influence the nature of the finished whisky. Malt-whisky distillers are conservative in many things, including the shape and size of the still: a new one is likely to be an exact replica of the old. Chemists have never been able to discover precisely what determines the special character of the product of each distillery or exactly why it is that maturing effects such an improvement in flavour. As a result, brewers and stillmen tend to have their own special mystique: theirs – to emphasize the point once again – is an art, in which instinct born of long (and often hereditary) experience plays its part. Bruce Lockhart has remarked that 'some brewers are so fearful of any change affecting their product that they will not allow even a cobweb to be swept away from the vat room'. One of the problems arises from the fact that until a whisky has matured it is impossible to be absolutely certain of its quality, though an experienced taster can hazard a shrewd guess. But we do know that the quality of the barley (even though, as we have seen, it does not have to be Scottish barley), the composition of the peat, and the quality of the water each has something to do with the quality of the finished whisky. Whiskies can be more or less heavily peated. Some have claimed that the best whisky is made from water which comes 'off granite through peat' and others that water 'off peat through granite' produces the better whisky. There is certainly a difference between the two. Heavy peating can be achieved by passing the peat smoke repeatedly over the malt in the drying kiln by means of fans. A growing number of distilleries no longer do their own malting, but buy their malt ready-made from maltsters, peated to the desired degree.

The malting process takes from nine to fifteen days; brewing and distilling together occupy one week, the first part of which is devoted to brewing and the latter part to continuous distilling. The new whisky comes from the spirit receiver at a strength of from 15° to 20° over proof (or 115° to 120° proof). At this point a digression on the nature and meaning of proof suggests itself, since I have found so many people confused about the exact meaning of the term. One of the meanings of the word 'proof' at least since the sixteenth century is 'of tried strength or quality' and it is this meaning that is involved in the phrase 'proof spirit', which simply means spirit of standard and approved strength. The problem for centuries has been what standard to require and how to define it. In earlier times the strength of a spirit was determined by very crude methods, such as dampening gunpowder with it and then applying a light to see if it would still ignite. The development of the hydrometer – a floating instrument used to determine the specific gravity (weight in relation to the weight of the same volume of water) of a liquid – led to less crude methods. After a great deal of research and calculation in a variety of countries, the British Government at the beginning of this century produced tables relating the strength of spirit to its specific gravity at 60° F. These tables have subsequently been amended, and definition of proof is based on the amended tables. The Customs and Excise Act of 1952 gave the following definition of proof spirit : 'Spirits shall be deemed to be at proof if the volume of the ethyl alcohol contained therein made up to the volume of the spirits with distilled water has a weight equal to that of twelve-thirteenths of a volume of distilled water equal to the volume of the spirits, the volume of each liquid being computed as at fifty-one degrees Fahrenheit.' Put less forbiddingly, this means that proof spirit is that which at 51° F. weighs twelve-thirteenths of an equal volume of water at the same temperature. The tables show how much alcohol and how much water the spirit will then contain, so that we can re-define proof, more usefully for the general reader, as spirit which contains 57·1 per cent of alcohol by volume or 49·28 per cent of alcohol by weight. Now, this is *British* proof. *American* proof is calculated differently. The standard of proof recognized by the United States is 50 per cent of alcohol by volume at 60° F. This means that British proof spirit (i.e. 100° proof) would be 114·2° proof in the United States (or 14·2° over proof). Similarly, American 100° proof is the same as British 87·7° proof. This difference is worth noting, because Scotch whisky for the American market is bottled at 76·2° proof (or 23·8° under proof) according to the British standard, but this corresponds to 86·8° on the American standard of proof and '86·8° proof' appears on American bottles of Scotch. Though this is stronger than the 70° proof at which most Scotch whisky is bottled for the domestic market, it is not as much stronger as Americans who see '70° proof' on British bottles of Scotch and '86·8°' on bottles of Scotch exported to America generally believe, for 70° proof on the British standard is the equivalent of 80° proof on the American standard. All this may sound tediously technical, but I have deliberately not relegated it to a footnote because whisky drinkers really ought to know what proof is and what the difference between British and American proof is. I have seen more than one American knock back Scotch whisky from a British bottle marked '70° proof' under the impression that it was in fact 16 degrees lower in proof than the whisky he was accustomed to drink at home. And one's belief can colour one's actual physical sensation in drinking, so that by misreading the label one can really believe one is drinking a much weaker spirit than one actually is. And the results of this can be awkward.[7]

Let us now return to the newly distilled whisky, which is from 115° to 120° proof. It is colourless, extremely pungent and fiery. From the spirit receiver it is run into the spirit store, where it is reduced in strength by the addition of spring water (and here again the quality of the water is important) to about 110° proof before being run into casks to mature.

Nobody knows precisely when it was first realized that whisky improves in a spectacular fashion when matured in

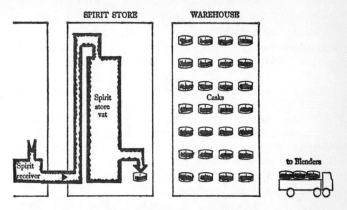

the wood, though French cognac distillers seem to have learned the advantages of maturing brandy in wood in the eighteenth century. Though I have met distillery workers who prefer the powerful new whisky straight from the still, there is no doubt at all that the characteristic qualities of a fine malt whisky require time to develop. Scotch whisky, in fact, is not (and has not been since 1915) legally Scotch whisky until it has been matured in a bonded warehouse in cask for at least three years.[8] But the whisky is still immature at three years, and five years would be a more appropriate minimum period. The rate of maturation depends in some measure on the size of the cask – the smaller the cask, the faster the maturing. Eight years in a quarter (a cask of 30 gallons or less) may be sufficient to produce a well-matured malt whisky; in a hogshead of 55 to 65 gallons ten years would be a more likely bet; in a butt of 110 gallons, twelve or fifteen years. Of course one can never tell for certain in advance when a whisky is going to be at its best. Up to a point, the longer it stays in the wood the better, but after fifteen years there is always the danger of the whisky acquiring a slightly 'woody' flavour, and in a small cask it may already have acquired a woodiness by its fifteenth year. The smaller the cask, the larger the amount of whisky lost through absorption by the porosity of the wood of the cask. This wood is oak, and oak with the proper degree of porosity, for the porosity (enabling the spirit to 'breathe' without leaking) is essential for the maturing process. Not only is there a loss of volume during maturation in oak casks; there is also a loss of strength. There is a popular belief that the longer a whisky is matured the stronger it will emerge, but this is quite wrong. The degree of humidity in the warehouse where the casks lie during the maturing process also affects the degree to which a maturing whisky loses both its volume and its strength : the greater the humidity the more it loses strength, and the drier the more it loses volume. It has been calculated that about four million gallons of Scotch whisky are lost each year through absorption or evaporation.

It has long been known that oak casks which have previously contained sherry give a splendid mellowing effect to the mature whisky. In 1864 William Sanderson (who later developed 'Vat 69' whisky) wrote that 'it is well-known that Whisky stored in Sherry casks soon acquires a mellow softness which it does not get when put into new casks; in fact the latter if not well seasoned, will impart a *woodiness* much condemned by the practised palate. In Sherry casks the spirit likewise acquires a pleasing tinge of colour which is much sought for.' It is the sherry, soaking back from the wood into the spirit, that traditionally has given Scotch whisky its golden colour. A cask that has held a pale sherry will impart a paler colour, and a delicate straw-coloured whisky will emerge. A cask that has held a dark sherry will impart a darker colour and a fuller flavour. (The sherry imparts a softness and sometimes, in whisky from a cask that has held dark sherry, just a whisper of sherry flavour. What is wanted, though, is not any flavour from the original sherry, rather a topping of smoothness and softness – but these are difficult things to describe.) Or one could use for a second time a sherry cask that had already been used once for maturing whisky : the 'refill' or 'second-fill' cask will impart a more delicate colouring than it imparted the first time.

Sherry casks have for long been in short supply (though

as I go round the distilleries my impression is that the situation is somewhat better than it has been), and many less satisfactory substitutes have been and are being employed. Of course, whisky can be matured in plain oak casks, emerging either colourless or the palest of straw colours, and I have tasted some truly great malt whiskies matured in this way. The whole question of the nature, origin and use of casks is worth detailed consideration, and since most casks today are owned by the blending firms – who send their casks up to be filled by the individual distilleries, where they are left to mature until needed – I reserve my discussion of this topic until I come to discuss blending. The same thing goes for the artificial colouring of whisky, which as a rule is done by the blenders.

Whisky is further reduced in proof by the addition of water before bottling, the strength at which it is bottled depending on the market for which it is intended. 70° proof is now normal for the home market, though stronger bottlings of some of the best malts are available. For the United States it is 76·2° proof (86·8° proof on the American standard). For general export markets the proof is 75·8°.

Whisky does not mature in the bottle, for the porosity of the cask is a significant factor in maturation. Yet clearly *something* happens if you keep whisky in the bottle for a very long time indeed. Neil Gunn tells of finding in Caithness in the early 1930s a bottle of whisky with a seal marked 'Scrabster 1830'. He tasted it with the direct intention of finding out what happened when whisky had been in the bottle for so long, and found that 'it had matured to an incredible smoothness' yet possessed 'an attractively objectionable flavour, somewhere between rum and tar'. He concluded that some soot must have fallen into the malt (he explained how this could have happened) which, in the whisky's extreme age, had become all-pervasive. Most of us have no opportunity of carrying out an experiment of this sort. It is best to assume that whisky matures only in the wood, and to drink it after it has been so matured for at least eight years.

So far I have been describing pot-still malt Scotch whisky,

the true, original whisky of Scotland. In a later chapter I shall have something to say about blended Scotch whiskies and about Lowland grain whisky which plays such an important part in modern blends. But now let us take a brief look at the different regions of Scotland where pot-still malt whisky is produced. (The reader can follow this by reference to the map in the Appendix.)

The traditional division of Scotch whisky is into Highland Malts, Lowland Malts, Campbeltowns and Islays. All are made in the manner described above, but they differ considerably in character.[9] The most famous of the Highland Malts are the Eastern Malts, most of which come from Banffshire and the areas adjoining it on the east (the western part of Aberdeenshire) and the west (Morayshire). The River Spey and its tributaries flow by some great distilleries, and Speyside has more distilleries to the square mile than any other part of Scotland. Indeed, that whole part of Scotland which lies just south of the Moray Firth – an area which, as I pointed out at the beginning of this chapter, includes a fertile coastal plain where barley is one of the crops grown, as well as mountains, valleys, streams and springs – is the country of the Eastern Malt. From Grantown-on-Spey to the Moray Firth coast on the north and to Huntly on the east (see the inset map) the landscape is thick with great distilleries. Glenlivet distillery, the most famous of all, lies eastward over the Hills of Cromdale from Strathspey, between the River Avon and the Livet Water, overlooking the latter, in beautiful countryside. If you go about ten miles up Glen Rinnes from Glenlivet (with Ben Rinnes on your left) you come to Dufftown, where distilleries cluster. I remember once fishing in the River Fiddich and looking across at Dufftown and seeing little else but the pagoda tops of distilleries. A little farther north, on the Spey at Craigellachie, farther west in Glen Rothes, and a bit north and west again around Elgin, there are further clusters of distilleries. But, though it is in these parts that we find the greatest concentration of distilleries, there are Eastern Malts somewhat farther afield : farther east, in Inverness-shire, across the Cromarty Firth in Ross-shire, farther north still in Brora, Sutherland, and even as far north as Wick. There are also distilleries westward in Fort William and in Oban and two in the Orkney Islands which have the qualities of Eastern Malts.

The Eastern Malts vary greatly among themselves, but in general it can be said that they are subtler and sometimes lighter than the Islays and Campbeltowns. From the full and sophisticated Glenlivet to the light yet peaty Tomatin, from the quietly rich Glen Mhor to the fragrant and delicate Glenmorangie, from the mellow and fruity Clynelish to the dry yet flowery Glenfiddich, Eastern Malts cover a wide range. Yet they are all different from a typical Islay whisky, which has a characteristic heaviness and peatiness (which makes it important in blending). The island of Islay with its eight distilleries lies in the Atlantic opposite Kintyre, a southward-jutting peninsula west of the Isle of Arran; in Kintyre is situated Campbeltown, a town once very famous for its numerous malt whisky distilleries. Now only two remain. Campbeltowns have in the past had something of the strength and body of Islays, and are indeed traditionally regarded as the most manly of whiskies. But of the two now distilled in Campbeltown, only one (Glen Scotia) lives up to the traditional description; the other (Springbank) is much lighter in body though agreeably full in flavour. So Campbeltowns, once a highly important category of Scotch whisky, no longer play a great part in the Scotch whisky scene. There is a single distillery on the Island of Skye, Talisker, which produces a whisky which belongs in general with the Islay and Campbeltown groups. (I have in fact seen Highland malt whisky classified simply as Eastern Malts and Western Malts, the latter including Islays, Campbeltowns and Talisker.)

Malt whisky is also distilled in the Lowlands, and has been since the eighteenth century. There are now ten Lowland malt distilleries, beside about a hundred Highland malt distilleries (including both the eastern and the western). Lowland Malts are distinctly lighter than Highland or Island malts. The association of Scotch whisky with the Highlands and the fact that the greatest of malt whiskies do come from Highland distilleries should not be allowed to obscure the real merits of good Lowland Malt whisky. But I discuss the qualities of individual malt whiskies in a later chapter. All of these whiskies – Highland Malts, Islays and Campbeltowns, and Lowland Malts – must be distinguished from a much later invention, grain whisky made not by the pot-still process but in a 'patent still'. But the first thing in any inquiry into Scotch whisky is to look at the pot-still malt whisky which is the true and original spirit of Scotland and still the basis of any whisky which properly calls itself Scotch, however much grain whisky it may be blended with. It is a spirit bound up for centuries with the social history of Scotland.

We have seen the reference to Friar John Cor and his eight bolls of malt in 1494. Two centuries later we find a reference to an 'usquebaugh' (an earlier form of the word 'whisky', intermediate between the Gaelic *uisge beatha* and the modern word) in Scotland that was not made of malt at all. Writing of the Island of Lewis, in the Hebrides, about 1695, Martin Martin observed that 'the air is temperately cold and moist, and for the corrective the natives use a dose of trestarig or usquebaugh'. The cereals grown on the island were barley, oats and rye : the islanders distilled a spirit from the first two, but apparently, and perhaps surprisingly in view of the history of rye whisky in North America, not from the third.[10] Their abundance of grain, wrote Martin, 'disposed the natives to brew several sorts of liquors, as common usquebaugh, another called trestarig, *id est*, aqua-vitae, three times distilled, which is strong and hot; a third is four times distilled, and this by the natives is called usquebaugh-baul, *id est*, usquebaugh, which at first taste affects all the members of the body :[11] two spoonfuls of this last liquor is a sufficient dose; and if any man exceed this, it would presently stop his breath, and endanger his life. The trestarig and usquebaugh-baul are both made of oats.'

Trestarig, which comes from two Gaelic words meaning 'triple strength', is thus not the true malt whisky, and neither is usquebaugh-baul. We know very little about either of these varieties of spirit. If you look up 'trestarig' in Jamieson's *Dictionary of the Scottish Language* you will find it defined as 'a kind of ardent spirits distilled from oats' and ascribed to the Isle of Lewis; but in fact the only reference given is to the passage from Martin I have just quoted. There were clearly other spirits distilled in seventeenth- and eighteenth-century Scotland besides malt liquor. A crude spirit distilled from a mash of oats and barley was not uncommon among tenant farmers of both the Highlands and the Lowlands. Yet it is clear that by the seventeenth century whisky was already established as the characteristic Highland spirit and that in the eighteenth, in spite of continuous troubles with the Excise after the failure of the 1745 rebellion, whisky distilling flourished in the Highlands and, with its product, spread into the Lowlands.

In the seventeenth and eighteenth centuries English writers associated 'usquebaugh' or whisky with both Ireland and Scotland. John Marston's play *The Malcontent*, probably written in 1602–3, has two characters sing this song:

> The Dutchman for a drunkard,
> The Dane for golden locks,
> The Irishman for usquebaugh,
> The Frenchman for the [pox].

Dr Johnson, who was not knowledgeable about whisky and tasted it for the first time on his Hebridean tour in 1773,[12] knew at least that the Irish and the Scotch varieties were different, though he expressed the difference rather oddly. In his *Dictionary* (1755) he defined 'usquebaugh' as 'a compounded distilled spirit, being drawn on aromaticks; and the Irish sort is particularly distinguished for its pleasant and mild flavour. The Highland sort is somewhat hotter; and by corruption, in Scottish they call it *whisky*.' The good Dr Jamieson, whose *Dictionary of the Scottish Language* I have already cited, was moved to protest against the older doctor's definition. *His* definition of 'whisky' reads: 'A species of ardent spirits, distilled from malt . . . I know not how the learned lexicographer had adopted the idea of its being drawn on aromatics, unless it had been from the occasional flavour of the *peat-reek*. Perhaps Dr Johnson meant *Bitters*, a dram much used in the Highlands as a stomachic, made from an infusion of aromatic herbs and whisky.' The 1775 enlarged edition of Nathaniel Bailey's *Universal Etymological English Dictionary* defined 'usquebeaugh' as 'a distilled Spirit made in *Ireland* and the Highlands of *Scotland* also called *Whisky*'. Bailey did not attempt to distinguish between the Irish and the Scotch varieties by flavour, nor did he made a distinction between Irish whisk*ey* and Scotch whisk*y*, which is a modern convention.

Jamieson's reference to whisky bitters reminds us that Scotch whisky was in earlier times used in ways that would make the modern connoisseur frown. Some of these ways will be discussed later, but at this point I pause only to reinforce Jamieson's conjecture about what Dr Johnson really meant with an anecdote recorded by Sir Archibald Geikie which shows that 'an infusion of aromatic herbs and whisky' remain common in the Highlands until well into the second half of the nineteenth century. Sir Archibald was staying at a cottage in Skye, and was awakened in the morning by the eldest daughter of the house with a request that he would 'taste something before he got up', to give him an appetite for breakfast. He declined and she insisted : 'Some whusky nate? Some whusky and wahtter? Some whusky and milk?[13] Some acetates?' The 'acetates', Geikie decided, must have been a 'decoction of bitter roots in whisky, often to be found on Highland sideboards in the morning'.

To whatever eccentric uses the malt whisky of Scotland was sometimes put, the fact that it was a life-enhancing spirit made from barley was established in the Scottish imagination well before the seventeenth century. Burns's ballad *John Barleycorn* is, as the poet himself acknowledged, a re-working of an old folk song telling of John Barleycorn's death (when the barley is cut) and eventual resurrection as a fermented liquor; but Burns clearly saw the product as a distilled liquor, whisky. There are curious sacramental overtones in the conception :

And they hae taen his very heart's blood,
    And drank it round and round;
And still the more and more they drank,
    Their joy did more abound.

John Barleycorn was a hero bold,
    Of noble enterprise;
For if you do but taste his blood,
    'Twill make your courage rise.

Social and Economic History to 1823

The production of Scotch whisky early attracted the attention of tax-hungry governments, and one could write a whole history of Scotch in terms of the taxes on it, their causes and consequences. The control of the production and consumption of potable spirits by taxation can be traced at least as far back as fourteenth-century Europe with the rise of brandy consumption in France and Germany. Heavy taxation in Germany as early as 1360 in order to control the *Schnapsteufel* or brandy-devil does not seem to have achieved this object. But since then governments have continued to regard potable spirits as an obvious target for taxation on the grounds that by taxing them one can simultaneously raise revenue and lessen drunkenness. There is also the sour view that products that add conspicuously to human joy ought to be strictly controlled. 'The best things in life are free', says the song, but governments are suspicious of this view and would probably tax sex if they could. As it is, sex remains on the whole a private and untaxed pleasure, whereas Scotch whisky, from being a widely dispersed domestic industry produced in or near farms and cottages and if not actually free at least very cheap, has under centuries of government pressure become the concern of large commercial enterprises and very expensive to the consumer. This change in scale of the production of whisky from a cottage industry to an industry consisting of much larger (and much more efficient) units was a process taking place throughout the eighteenth century, with the Government devising its tax laws so as to force whisky production into fewer and larger (and so more easily controllable) units and the public resisting by dispersing illicit stills in inaccessible spots all over the country, especially, of course, the Highlands. This is part of a larger pattern of economic development throughout Britain, a pattern which becomes even more distinct in the nineteenth century, when the production of whisky becomes increasingly rationalized and commercialized. One must not get too sentimental over these changes : most of them were inevitable, many (but not all) of them resulted in the long run in the improvement of the quality of the large mass of whisky distilled and all of them helped to extend the whisky-drinking habit far beyond Scotland.

Accounts of changing tax laws are one of the more tedious kinds of history, and I do not propose to weary the reader with the details of duty levied on Scotch at different times. But the main outline of the story is of some interest, and helps to explain a great deal in the history of Scotch. An excise tax on spirits was imposed by the Scots Parliament in 1644; it was lowered under Cromwell (thus exploding any facile theory about the relation of Puritanism to drinking), lapsed after the Restoration in 1660, and was reimposed in 1693. In 1707, the year of the Union between England and Scotland, the Board of Excise was established, and it was clear that the whisky duty was here to stay. In 1713 what was now the British Parliament (for the independent Scots Parliament vanished in 1707) decided to impose the English malt tax in Scotland, but kept it at half the English tax. In spite of this concession the new malt tax was intensely unpopular in Scotland, and caused riots in Edinburgh and Glasgow. It also both encouraged the development of illicit stills — which existed in large quantities all over the Highlands — and made certain that illicit whisky was of better quality than that legally distilled since the legal distillers, to minimize the malt tax, used a high proportion of raw grain with only enough malted barley to ensure the saccharification of the grain by the diastase of malt. Thus illegally distilled whisky was the more likely to be the genuine Highland malt Scotch whisky.

There was one famous still which remained legally tax-free until 1786. The story is well told in the elegant language of Mr Robert Forsyth in the fifth volume of his 'clear and full account' of Scotland and her resources published under the title *The Beauties of Scotland* in 1805 :

The small village of Fairntosh [or Ferintosh, in Ross-shire] only deserves notice on account of a singular privilege which its proprietor, Forbes of Culloden, long enjoyed. At the time of the revolution, in 1688, Mr Forbes of Culloden was a zealous whig, in consequence of which his estates were laid waste, particularly the barony of Fairntosh, on which extensive distilleries belonging to him were destroyed. As a compensation, the parliament of Scotland granted to him, in 1690, freedom from excise for these lands, on condition that he should make an annual payment of 400 merks Scots. The proprietors of this estate continued extremely loyal. The son of the grantee of this privilege, in 1715, raised in arms all the men upon his estate for the support of the Hanoverian succession; and the succeeding proprietor, in 1745, being then Lord President of the Court of Session, contributed greatly to prevent the extension of the rebellion, and prevailed with some of the most powerful chieftains to remain quiet. The privilege was, in 1786, resumed by government, and the sum of L.20,000 was granted as a compensation to the proprietor. Before that period Fairntosh whisky was much relished in Scotland; it had a strong flavour of the smoke of the peat with which the malt of which it was made was dried; but this was considered as one of the marks of its being genuine.

It was in fact an act of 1785 (not 1786) dealing with the Scottish distilleries that abolished the Ferintosh privilege. Forbes was not satisfied with the original sum offered him by way of compensation, and the case was decided by a jury before the Scottish Court of Exchequer on 29 November 1785. Forbes's counsel, the great whig politician Henry Erskine, argued that the potential yield to the Forbes family was £7000 a year and also that the late Duncan Forbes had spent £20,000 of his own fortune in helping to suppress the rebellion of 1745–6. The jury awarded the sum of £21,580. Forbes was happy, but young Robert Burns, as yet unknown but in the midst of an *annus mirabilis* of poetic energy and production, was not:

Thee, Ferintosh! O sadly lost!
Scotland lament frae coast to coast!
Now colic grips, an' barkin hoast   *cough*
      May kill us a';
For loyal Forbes' chartered boast
      Is taen awa!

Thae curst horse-leeches o' th' Excise,
Wha mak the whisky stells their prize!
Haud up thy han', Deil! ance, twice, thrice!
      There, seize the blinkers!   *spies*
An' bake them up in brunstane pies
      For poor damn'd drinkers.

Later on Burns himself was to become an exciseman, but here his sympathies, like those of the majority of the Scottish people, were with the illicit distillers and against the inspectors and tax gatherers. It was the aftermath of the Forty-five that did the real damage. The British Government were determined that never again should rebellion come down from the Highlands and they set about the occupation and domination of all Scotland north of the Highland line. True, after the Union of 1707 English revenue officers had appeared in Scotland to administer a system of taxation involving an obligation on the part of each distiller to produce a specified amount of whisky out of each hundred gallons of wash and a deficiency payment on the total output if this amount was not reached. But before General Wade's roads (1726–33) the Highlands were virtually impassable, and before the defeat of the Jacobite rebellion of 1745 the Highlanders, even with Wade's roads available, were still left very much to themselves. And, of course, vast areas still remained difficult if not impossible of access to those not familiar with the territory. And it was just these difficult areas – the remote glens and hillsides – which provided the best conditions for the distillation of malt whisky. The taxation of whisky in the first half of the eighteenth century was not really a serious matter; such taxation as was imposed was not savage, and it was often enough evaded by illicit distillers. It was not only in the Highlands that illicit distilling was carried on. Edinburgh in 1777 had eight licensed and, according to the excise officers, 400 illicit stills. Legal Lowland distillers (who often produced inferior whisky for the reasons explained above) complained bitterly about competition from illegal stills. Illicit Highland whisky was smuggled into the Lowlands and into England.

The Government was nonplussed by the whole situation. After innumerable reports, discussions, protests by English distillers (of gin) against the more favourable rate of taxation applied to Scotland, commissions of inquiry and debates, the Wash Act of 1784 was passed. This Act drew a formal distinction between the Lowlands and the Highlands, and in the latter duty was to be charged not on the amount of whisky produced but on the capacity of the still. In the Lowlands the tax was 5*d* per gallon on the wash, on the assumption that 100 gallons of wash would yield 20 gallons of spirit; in the Highlands all stills had to pay a licence duty of 20*s* per gallon of still content. The Highland line, which separated the two forms of duty, was precisely defined in the Act – the first time that a specified area of Scotland was separated from the rest as the Highlands by Act of Parliament.

But the Wash Act did not work as it was supposed to work. The Government had assumed that, by restricting the size of the Highland still, they would restrict to a predictable quantity the amount produced. But the ingenuity of the distillers found ways of speeding up the process of distilling so as to produce much more in a given period than the authorities had worked out that they would or could. The Scotch Distillery Act of 1786 applied to all Scotland; it increased the tax to £1 10*s* per gallon of still content (considered the equivalent of 6*d* on the gallon of whisky actually produced) and added an extra 2*s* per gallon for whisky imported into England to bring the duty into line with the English tax of 2*s* 6*d* per gallon on spirits. This, of course, increased smuggling across the Border into England. It also gave a further impetus to the Scottish distillers to work out improvements which would enable them to increase their rate of production. Further increases in the rate of duty followed, in an attempt by the Government to compensate for this, but this in turn further stimulated the ingenuity of the distillers. In 1788 an additional duty of 6*d* per gallon was imposed on whisky sent to England, and this gravely damaged the trade of the Lowland distillers, James and John Haig of Canonmills, Edinburgh, and bankrupted James and John Stein of Kilbagie and Kennetpans, Clackmannanshire, who had specialized in exports to London. (We shall hear more later of those two important whisky families, the Haigs and the Steins.)

All the time illicit distilling went on merrily in the Highlands. There, John Stein said in his evidence before the Committee on Distilleries (1798), 'the distillery is in a thousand hands. It is not confined to great towns or to regular manufacturers, but spreads itself over the whole face of the country, and in every island from the Orkneys to Jura. There are many who practise this art who are ignorant of every other, and there are distillers who boast that they make the best possible Whiskey who cannot read or write, and who carry on this manufacture in parts of the country where the use of the plough is unknown, and where the face of an Exciseman was never seen. Under such circumstances, it is impossible to take account of its operations; it is literally to search for revenue in the woods or on the mountains.' The legal distiller found it hard to compete.

To the Highlander illicit distilling was no crime. For generations he had used his barley, his water and his peat to make his national drink, and he could not see why any government should interfere. Men of the highest moral character, including highly religious men and even ministers (though some ministers deplored the consumption of whisky) regarded illicit distilling and smuggling as proper and even necessary activities. The necessity lay in the fact that since tenant farmers found their rent money from the produce of their farms, it was often only by converting their barley into whisky that they could find enough money to pay their rent. Again and again, in reading through the *Statistical*

Account of Scotland (that invaluable economic and social survey of Scotland produced in the 1790s, parish by parish, by the parish ministers) we find this point made. In a final desperate measure to control distilling in the Highlands, the Government by an Act of 1814 prohibited, within the Highland line, all stills of less than 500 gallons capacity and at the same time substituted for all former duties one of 1s per gallon of wort together with 2s 10d per gallon of spirit; and 18 gallons of spirit were required to be produced from each 100 gallons of wort.

The setting of the minimum size of the Highland still as 500 gallons capacity was unrealistic and indeed fantastic. 'It was evident,' wrote Colonel Stewart of Garth (the man who supervised George IV's Highland dress on the King's visit to Scotland in 1822), 'that this law was a complete interdict, as a still of this magnitude would consume more than the disposable grain in the most extensive county within this newly drawn boundary; nor could fuel be obtained for such an establishment without an expense which the community could not possibly bear. The sale, too, of the spirits produced was circumscribed within the same line, and thus the market which alone could have supported the manufacture was entirely cut off.' More than ever illicit distilling came to be the only way in which many Highlanders could sell their surplus barley in such a way as would enable them to pay their rents. The confusion resulting from the 1814 Act finally led to the much more reasonable legislation of 1823 which, as we shall see, had momentous consequences for the future of Scotch whisky.

The Reverend Mr·David Dunoon, minister of the parish of Killearnan in Ross-shire, gave a detailed account of the legal distilleries in his parish for the seventeenth volume of the *Statistical Account*, published in 1796. He concluded:

It will be asked, Why then so many distilleries? For these reasons: Distilling is almost the only method of converting our victual into cash for the payment of rent and servants; and whisky may, in fact, be called our staple commodity. The distillers do not lay the proper value on their time and trouble, and of course look on all, but the price of the barley and the fire added to the tax, as clear profit; add to these the luxury of tasting the quality of the manufacture during the process.

'The distillers do not lay the proper value on their time and trouble.' They *enjoyed* making whisky, in fact, and did not consider that they should be paid for their time while so employed. Is this one clue to the uniqueness of Highland malt whisky – that it can only be made in Scotland by people who actively enjoy making it?

The views on whisky expressed by the parish ministers who wrote for the *Statistical Account* are interestingly varied, but again and again the matter of payment of rent is mentioned. The Reverend Mr John Downie of Urray (Presbytery of Dingwall, Synod of Ross) has this to say (volume VII, 1793):

A sense of religion and decency prevails among the people in general. One man only, within the memory of tradition, was convicted of a capital crime, and suffered for it about 50 years ago. No doubt, such a number engaged in distilling spirits, has a tendency to corrupt the morals; but the bad effects of this trade are less discernible than might be feared. Were the effects worse than they are, there is a fatal necessity of continuing the distillery, until some other manufacture be established in its stead, whereby the people will be enabled to find money to pay their rents. The worst effect of the great plenty of spirits is, that dram shops are set up in almost every village for retail, where young and idle people convene and get drunk. These tipling huts are kept by such only as are not able to pay a fine, or procure a licence. They are the greatest nuisance in the parish. It is a pity that no effectual mode has yet been effected for suppressing them.

The account of the parish of King-Edward (Presbytery of Turriff, County and Synod of Aberdeen) is, unusually, written by the parish schoolmaster, Alexander Simpson, not by the minister. Writing in volume XI (1794), he applauds 'the small licensed whisky stills in the neighbourhood'. Not only do they 'afford a good market for barley', he says, but they also supply 'us with good whisky, of a quality greatly superior to what we have from the large stills in the southern districts, as well as cheaper, and no less wholesome than foreign spirits'. These stills, he concludes, 'in every point of view, are a reciprocal advantage to the farmers, and the country at large'. Clearly the dominie's view of the benefits of whisky is more favourable than the minister's – or is it that the dominie can speak out more frankly on the matter?

Campbeltown, on the southern end of the peninsula of Kintyre, Argyllshire, had thirty-two distilleries at the end of the eighteenth century. It was for long one of the great homes of whisky, and produced a variety of western malts of great distinction, known and distinguished as Campbeltowns. Twenty years ago there were only four distilleries left there; now there are but two. But in 1794 the Reverend Mr John Smith, writing in the tenth volume of the *Statistical Account*, had a great deal to say about the distilleries there:

Next to the fishing of herrings, the business most attended to in Campbelton is the distilling of whisky; which the following is the state for the present year.

	No. of Stills	Bolls distilled	Produce in Gall.
In the town	22	5500	19800
In the country	10	2134	6350
	32	7634	26150

But the Reverend Mr John Smith took no pleasure in contemplating the flourishing whisky industry in his parish. 'This business is undoubtedly gainful to a few individuals, but extremely ruinous to the community,' he wrote. 'It consumes their means, hurts their morals, and destroys both their undertakings and their health. Were it not for preventing the temptation of smuggling, a duty next to a prohibition would be *mercy*.' He goes on to point out that one can get completely drunk for 2*d* or 3*d*. But, surprisingly, he adds : 'In this place, however, very few, comparatively speaking, are given to drunkenness, as people are seldom given to excess in what is their daily fare.' No, it is not drunkenness, he continues, that is the trouble, but something else :

. . . the trade, when carried on to such an extent, is extremely hurtful to this parish in another point of view. To it we owe the want of wheat or flour of our own, which takes yearly out of the place about 2000 *l.*; besides the want of a sufficiency of meal to serve the inhabitants, for which we send away about as much more. Both these sums might be saved, if we could be kept from destroying so much of our own and our neighbours grain. But the prospect of enormous gain, first tempts the indigent to convert their little crop into a pernicious liquor, and then the law obliges them to drink it themselves, as it cannot be sold but where they have equal poverty and equal liberty. Thus, in the trite story, two publicans, who went alternately to each others houses, with the same twopence, drank both their cellars dry. Were we allowed to export a part, to help us pay our meal and flour, it would do us much service. We have, however, much cause to be thankful for the present law, as it stands; for it has been productive of much good to the country. It has put the business into few hands, and therefore removed from many a temptation, too strong for their feeble virtue. It has happily put an end to smuggling; and, as we must have some liquor, it makes us drink our own, and allows us to drink it better, than when it was made clandestinely and imperfectly. The revenue too has been raised since, by our collector (Mr Mackenzie), to full four times what it was before the act took place; and the farmer gets a better price, and better payment, for his grain.

Before we leave the *Statistical Account* (which is packed with information about whisky in late eighteenth-century

Scotland), let us look at the report from a Lowland parish where highly commercialized distilling went on largely for the London market until stopped by the special tax imposed in 1788 on whisky sent to England. The Reverend Mr Robert Moodie, minister of the Parish of Clackmannan in the County of Clackmannan, reports with expert knowledge in volume XIV (1795) on the great distilleries in his parish:

The two great distilleries of Kilbagie and Kennetpans are both in the parish of Clackmannan; and, previous to the year 1788, the manufacture of Scotch spirits was carried on at them to an extent hitherto unknown in this part of the island of Great Britain. The distillery laws have undergone various changes in Scotland. Before the year 1784, the duty was levied by a presumptive charge upon the wash (that is, fermented worts), taking it for granted, that the wash would produce one-fourth part in low wines, and that these low wines would produce three-fifths parts in spirits: hence, 100 gallons of wash was supposed to yield 15 gallons of spirits, and duty was charged accordingly; but instead of 15, 20 gallons of spirits were often drawn from the 100 of wash. In Scotland, the surplus above 15 gallons was uniformly seized, as spirits presumed to be fraudulently obtained; while in England the distiller was allowed the full exercise of his genius, and got permits for the removal of his actual produce. At this period, the quantum of duty on a gallon of spirits was more than double of what it has been ever since. But the high rate of duty afforded such temptation to smuggling, that the consumption of spirits in Scotland was chiefly supplied by the manufacture of illegal stills, and by smuggling from abroad. Great distillers could not smuggle; and being continually subjected to the surveys of the excise, the two distilleries of Kilbagie and Kennetpans depended entirely on the London market for the sale of their produce; where, previous to the year 1784, they carried on an advantageous trade: though the duty on a gallon of spirits in England was 13⅔ pence higher than in Scotland;[14] and though they had, at shipping their spirits for England, to pay down this difference on every gallon shipped. In

1784, a law was passed, rendering the duties, and mode of levying them, the same both in Scotland as in England; and at the same time reducing the rate of duty on each gallon about half of what it had been formerly; while it allowed the manufacturer a credit for 20 gallons of spirits from the 100 gallons of wash, and granted permits accordingly. The London distillers expected, that by this equalization plan, the Scotch could not continue their trade in London, and pay the duties in the same manner with themselves. But in this they were mistaken; for the trade increased. And it is the opinion of the best informed distillers, that the London distillers are not a match for the Scotch under an equal law. This mode was continued till July 1786, when the license act took place, imposing 30s a gallon yearly on the contents of every still used for distillation in Scotland; continuing the last plan with respect to England (where the duty amounted to 2s 6d for the gallon of spirits) and imposing an additional duty of 2s on the gallon of spirits sent from Scotland to England : which additional duty was to be paid in London, on the arrival of the spirits in the river Thames. This act was passed as an experiment, and was to continue for two years. Under it, the London distillers expected that the Scotch could not continue the trade to London. This trade, however, still continued to increase; which increased also the astonishment of the London traders, who gave in a representation to the Treasury upon the subject. In consequence of which, and upwards of six months previous to the natural expiration of the law, another law was passed, imposing a duty of 6d a gallon on all Scotch spirits sent to England, in addition to the former 2s; while the duty on spirits manufactured in England was allowed to remain at the 2s 6d. When this act was passed, the Scotch distilleries stopped payment. The law continued in this way till July 1788, when the licence duty in Scotland was doubled, and made 3l a gallon on the contents of the still; and at the same time laying the trader under such restrictions, when he worked for England, as to amount to a prohibition against his entering that market. And in July 1793, the licence has been raised to 9l Sterling a gallon yearly. Previous to the year 1788, the quantity of corn used annually at the distillery of Kilbagie alone, amounted to above 60,000 bolls, and the annual quantity of spirits made, to above 3000 tons. The black cattle fed annually were about 7000; swine 2000. The cattle were sold to butchers, who drove them to the Edinburgh and Glasgow markets; the swine were killed and cured into bacon and pork for England. The work people employed were nearly 300. The distillery and utensils cost upwards of 40,000*l* Sterling; and when sold by the trustee for the creditors of the former proprietor, yielded about 7000*l* Sterling.

No situation could have been more eligible for a distillery than Kilbagie; and it was erected in the most substantial manner. The buildings occupy a space of above 4 acres of ground; all surrounded by a high wall. The barns for malting are of a prodigious size, and are 4 stories in height. A small rivulet runs through the middle of the works, and drives a threshing mill, and all the grinding mills necessary for the distillery; besides supplying with water a canal, which communicates with the river Forth, of about a mile in length, cut for the purpose of conveying both the imports and exports of the distillery.

The distillery at Kennetpans, which is advantageously situated on the very banks of the river Forth, was in proportion to that of Kilbagie, as three to five. And before these two distilleries were stopped, they paid to government an excise duty considerably greater than the whole land tax of Scotland. At present, the duty paid by both is about 8000*l* Sterling yearly. There is an engine, of Bolton and Watt's construction, at the distillery of Kennetpans; being the first of its kind that was erected in Scotland.

One can sense the Reverend Mr Moodie's pride as one reads his account of John Stein's two great Clackmannan distilleries, and his anger that London interests prevailed on the Government to alter the tax on Scottish spirits in such a way as to discourage exports to England. It is clear from his picture that there were relatively substantial exports of Scotch whisky from Scotland to England in the latter part of the eighteenth century, until the Act of 1788 which so damaged the Haigs and the Steins; and indeed we know this from other sources. These exports were mostly of Lowland malt whisky[15] (though I suspect that the spirit distilled at Kilbagie and Kennetpans was not always a pure malt spirit), which again in the nineteenth century was to come in quantity into the English market. But the really massive conquest of the English market, which involved quantities of quite different dimensions, was to await the invention of the Coffey still and the resulting blends of malt and grain whiskies developed by the whisky magnates of the latter part of the nineteenth century.

It is worth mentioning that whisky from the distillery at Kilbagie was well known to Robert Burns, who noted that it was 'much used as a beverage, morning, noon and night in Poosie Nansie's'. Poosie Nansie's was the pub in Mauchline where Burns set his low-life cantata, *The Jolly Beggars.* The tinker's song refers explicitly to it :

> Despise that shrimp, that wither'd imp,
>   With a' his nose an' cap'rin,
> An' take a share wi' those that bear
>   The budget and the apron!
> And by that stowp, my faith an' houpe!   *pot*
>   And by that dear Kilbaigie!
> If e'er ye want, or meet wi' scant,
>   May I ne'er weet my craigie!   *throat*

I have already suggested that I doubt whether Kilbagie consistently produced a purely malt whisky. Certainly the Haig distillery at Canonmills (and John Haig, who opened the Canonmills distillery in 1782, had learned all about distilling as an apprentice at the Kilbagie distillery, owned by his maternal grandfather John Stein) sometimes used rye and even wheat with the barley. We know this because when a hungry mob attacked the Canonmills distillery in June 1784, having heard that oats and potatoes were being used for distilling and thus were not available for food, Haig issued a statement in which he explained that he did not use these foodstuffs. 'It has unhappily taken possession of the minds of many people,' Haig's statement went, 'that all sorts of grain, wheat, oats, barley and pease, are there consumed in great quantities, and that even oat-meal and roots, such as potatoes, turnips, and carrots are made to serve the purposes of distillation; and, consequently, that the markets are really affected by this supposed consumption. Now, the genuine truth is, that no other species of grain are made use of at Canonmills but barley, rye, and sometimes such parcels of wheat as happen to receive damage, or are in quality unfit for bread; and that not a grain of oats, pease, or a particle of oat-meal, nor any potatoes, carrots, turnips or other roots, are used in the distillery in any shape.'

Burns, as every schoolboy knows, liked his dram, but he did not think much of the whisky distilled in the Lowlands. In a letter written on 22 December 1788 he thanks a friend for sending him a cask of what appears to have been High- land malt whisky, saying, 'It will bear five waters, strong; or six, ordinary Toddy.' He added: 'The Whisky of this country [i.e. region] is a most rascally liquor; and by con- sequence, only drank by the most rascally part of the inhabitants.' Perhaps the eighteenth-century English dis- tillers were right to rectify the whisky they bought from Stein and Haig and turn it into gin! (No reflection, I hasten to add, on the modern blended Haig Scotch whisky, one of the most interesting of the blended Scotches.)

It was in the eighteenth century that Scotch whisky ceased to be an almost exclusively Highland drink and became increasingly popular in the Lowlands after the middle of the century. The consumption of ale diminished as that of whisky increased. Many of the parish ministers who wrote in the *Statistical Account* referred to the increase of whisky consumption at the expense of ale, and some deplored this. According to the Reverend Mr Francis Forbes of Grange, Banffshire, the heavy excise tax on malt inevitably produced illicit distilling and smuggling and discouraged the brewing of beer (also made from malted barley).

In the earlier part of the eighteenth century English

travellers noted that whisky was a peculiarly Highland drink. 'The Landlord not only sits down with you, as in the northern Lowlands' – wrote Captain Edward Burt, on General Wade's staff in the Highlands in 1724–8 – 'but in some little time asks Leave (and sometimes not) to introduce his Brother, Cousin, or more, who are all to drink your Honour's Health in *Usky*; which, tho' a strong Spirit, is to them like Water. And this I have often seen 'em drink out of a Scollop Shell.' In the same account (*Letters from a Gentleman in the North of Scotland to His Friend in London*, 1754) the writer gives us some idea of how whisky was transported in the Highlands :

. . . In about three Hours after my Arrival at this Hut [a 'publick Hut' which served as a primitive inn] there appear'd on the other Side of the Water a Parcel of Merchants, with little Horses loaded with Roundlets of *Usky*.

Within Sight of the Ford was a Bridge (as they call'd it) made for the Convenience of this Place. It was compos'd of two small Fir-Trees not squared at all, laid one beside the other, across a narrow Part of the River, from Rock to Rock. There were Gaps and Intervals between those Trees, and beneath a most tumultuous Fall of Water.

Some of my Merchants bestriding the Bridge, edg'd forwards, and mov'd the Usky Vessels before 'em; but the others afterwards, to my Surprize, walk'd over this dangerous Passage, and dragg'd their *Garrons* through the Torrent, while the poor little Horses were almost drown'd with the Surge.

The writer has also something to say about the quantity of whisky drunk :

Some of the Highland Gentlemen are immoderate Drinkers of Usky, even three or four Quarts at a Sitting; and in general, the People that can pay the Purchase, drink it without Moderation.

Not long ago, four *English* Officers took a Fancy to try

their Strength in this Bow of *Ulysses*, against a like Number of Country Champions, but the Enemy came off victorious; and one of the Officers was thrown into a Fit of the Gout, without Hopes; another had a most dangerous Fever, a third lost his Skin and Hair by the Surfeit, and the last confessed to me, that when Drunkenness and Debate ran high, he took several Opportunities to sham it.

They say for Excuse, the Country requires a great deal; but I think mistake a Habit and Custom for Necessity. They likewise pretend it does not intoxicate in the Hills as it would do in the low Country, but this I also doubt by their own Practice; for those among them who have any Consideration will hardy care so much as to refresh themselves with it, when they pass near the Tops of the Mountains; for in that Circumstance, they say, it renders them careless, listless of the Fatigue, and inclined to sit down, which might invite to Sleep, and then they would be in Danger to perish with Cold . . . The Collector of the Customs at *Stornway* in the Isle of *Lewis* told me, that about 120 Families drink yearly 4000 *English* Gallons of this Spirit, and Brandy together, although many of them are so poor they cannot afford to pay for much of either, which you know must encrease the Quantity drank by the rest, and that they frequently give to Children, of six or seven Years old, as much at a time as an ordinary Wine-glass will hold.

When they chuse to qualify it for Punch they sometimes mix it with Water and Honey, or with Milk and Honey; at other times the Mixture is only the *Aqua Vitae*, Sugar and Butter, this they burn till the Butter and Sugar are dissolved.

The reference to brandy reminds us that imported (often smuggled) French brandy was also commonly drunk among Highland gentlemen, though our travelling Englishman was almost certainly wrong in suggesting that brandy was drunk at all by the poor. Later in the century, when whisky was becoming increasingly popular in the Lowlands, patriots exalted its claims against those of usurping brandy. The poet Robert Fergusson wrote in 1773 *A Drink Eclogue*, a dialogue between 'Landlady, Brandy and Whisky' in which Brandy attacks Whisky as a 'cottar loun' drunk by humble porters and 'chairmen' from the Highlands and asks indignantly:

> Ha'e ye nae breeding, that you shaw your nose
> Anent my sweetly gusted cordial dose.

Whisky laments the snobbery which makes people prefer foreign spirits:

> Alake! the byword's o'er weel kend throughout,
> 'Prophets at hame are held in nae repute';
> Sae fair'st wi' me, tho' I can heat the skin,
> And set the saul upon a merry pin,
> Yet I am hameil, there's the sour mischance!   *home-bred*
> I'm no frae Turkey, Italy, or France; ...

More than twenty years later Burns, in his poem *Scotch Drink*, praised whisky as the great native drink and attacked brandy —

> Wae worth that brandy, burnin trash!

In another poem written about the same time Burns addressed 'the Scotch representatives in the House of Commons' in a complaint about the taxation of whisky, ending with a 'Postscript' which is a great paean of praise to whisky, with the famous conclusion:

> Scotland, my auld, respected mither!
> Tho' whiles ye moistify your leather,   *sometimes*
> Till whare ye sit on craps o' heather
>   Ye tine your dam,   *lose; water*
> Freedom and whisky gang thegither,
>   Tak aff your dram!

The English traveller's reference to punch is important: though Highlanders generally drank their whisky neat, and though whisky connoisseurs today like their malt whisky neat or with a little water, whisky toddy was a common drink in eighteenth-century Scotland, especially in the Lowlands from the middle of the century. The traditional recipe for toddy involves whisky, sugar and hot water. The tumbler must be heated before the lump sugar is put in and dissolved in a glassful of boiling water. When the sugar is melted, add half a glass of whisky; stir with a silver spoon. The chief use of toddy in modern times is to relieve the symptoms of a cold. There used to be an elaborate ritual in both making and drinking toddy.

Toddy was drunk by gentlemen, but in the latter half of the eighteenth century in the Lowlands – as Fergusson's poem makes clear – neat whisky was more often the poor man's drink. Claret was the great drink of the Edinburgh 'literati', and many of them drank enormous quantities of it. They might drink toddy, or rum punch (the great drink of the Glasgow merchants trading with the West Indies) late in the evening, but were not as a rule serious dram-takers. Whisky in the Highlands was always a classless drink; in the Lowlands, once it became at all common, it was the democratic drink, the people's drink ('Freedom and whisky gang thegither!'), later, amid the squalid horrors that the Industrial Revolution left in its wake, often the only comfort of the destroyed and desperate; then high taxation put it virtually beyond the reach of the common man.

Whisky in the Highlands had its ritual and sacramental uses as well as satisfying daily needs. It was the standard drink at funerals. ('The ceremony [of burial] was closed with the discharge of pistols; then we returned to the castle, resumed the bottle, and by midnight there was not a sober person in the family, the females excepted. The 'squire and I were, with some difficulty, permitted to retire with our land lord in the evening; but our entertainer was a little chagrined at our retreat; and afterwards seemed to think it a disparagement to his family, that not above a hundred gallons of whisky had been drank upon such a solemn occasion.' Jery Melford's description of an Argyllshire funeral in Smollett's *Humphry Clinker*, 1770.) Whisky is still the funeral drink in the Highlands. Sir Archibald **Geikie** recorded an incident from the nineteenth century : he asked a girl if her aunt, who was gravely ill, was still living, and received the reply, 'Ay. She's no deid yet; but we've gotten in the whusky for the funeral.'

But, especially in the Highlands, it did not need a funeral to produce the whisky. Elizabeth Grant of Rothiemurchus, looking back in old age on Highland customs she had observed at the beginning of the nineteenth century, remarked on the perpetual whisky drinking :

The cheer she [Mrs Macintosh, 'a tidy guid-wife'] offered us was never more than bread and cheese and whisky . . . the whisky was a bad habit, there was certainly too much of it going. At every house it was offered, at every house it must be tasted or offence would be given, so we were taught to believe. I am sure now that had we steadily refused compliance with so incorrect a custom it would have been far better for ourselves, and might all the sooner have put a stop to so pernicious a habit among the people. Whisky-drinking was and is the bane of that country; from early morning till late at night it went on. Decent gentlewomen began the day with a dram. In our house the bottle of whisky, with its accompaniment of a silver salver full of small glasses, was placed on the side-table with cold meat every morning. In the pantry a bottle of whisky was the allowance per day, with bread and cheese in any required quantity, for such messengers or visitors whose errands sent them in that direction. The very poorest cottages could offer whisky; all the men engaged in the wood manufacture drank it in goblets three times a day, yet except at a merry-making we never saw any one tipsy.

In another passage Elizabeth Grant gives an account of the drinking habits of the loggers and their families :

The Spey floaters lived mostly down near Ballindalloch, a certain number of families by whom the calling had been followed for ages, to whom the wild river, all its holes and shoals and ricks and shiftings, were as well known as had its bed been dry. They came up in the season, at the first hint of a *spate*, as a rise in the water was called. A large bothy was built for them at the mouth of the Druin in a fashion that suited themselves; a fire on a hearth stone in the middle of the floor, a hole in the very centre of the roof just over it where some of the smoke got out, heather spread on the ground, no window, and there, after their hard day's work, they lay down for the night, in their wet clothes — for they had been perhaps hours on the river — each man's feet to the fire, each man's plaid round his chest, a circle of wearied bodies half stupified by whisky, enveloped in a cloud of steam and smoke, and sleeping soundly till the morning. They were a healthy race, suffering little except in their old age from rheumatism . . .

. . . When the men met in the morning they were supposed to have breakfasted at home, and perhaps they had had their private dram, it being cold work in a dark wintry dawn, to start over the moor for a walk of some miles to end in standing up to the knees in water; yet on collecting, whisky was always handed round; a lad with a small cask — a quarter anker — on his back, and a horn cup in his hand that held a gill, appeared three times a day among them. They all took their 'morning' raw, undiluted and without accompaniment, so they did the gill at parting when the work was done; but the noontide dram was part of a meal. There was a twenty minutes' rest from labour, and a bannock and a bit of cheese taken out of every pocket to be eaten leisurely with the whisky. When we were there the horn cup was offered first to us, and each of us took a sip to the health of our friends around us, who all stood up. Sometimes a floater's wife or bairn would come with a message; such messenger was always offered whisky. Aunt Mary had a story that one day a woman with a child in her arms, and another bit thing at her knee, came up among them; the horn cup was duly handed to her, she took a 'gey guid drap' herself, and then gave a little to each of the babies. 'My goodness, child,' said my mother to the wee thing that was trotting by the mother's side, 'doesn't it *bite* you?' 'Ay, but I like the bite,' replied the creature.

Whisky was in fact given to new-born infants in the Highlands, but just a spoonful. Elizabeth Grant's little brother William was given at his birth a spoonful of gin by his nurse instead, 'to test the strength of the young heir'.

There are numerous anecdotes of illicit distilling and whisky smuggling in the eighteenth and early nineteenth centuries. Looking back in her *Autobiography* on her summers spent at Park Hall, near Balfron, Stirlingshire, in the years 1813–17, Mrs Eliza Fletcher recalled :

Balfron was a most lawless village. There was a cotton mill in it, and the workers in it were among the best people there. It was illicit distillation that demoralised the district. The men of the place resorted to the woods or to the sequestered glens among the Campsie Hills, and there distilled whisky, which their wives and daughters took in tin vessels in the form of stays buckled round their waists to sell for a high price at Glasgow.

Thomas Guthrie recalled in his *Autobiography* the smugglers of his native Brechin when he was a boy there about the same time :

When a boy in Brechin [he was born in 1803], I was quite familiar with the appearance and on-goings of the Highland smugglers. They rode on Highland ponies, carrying on each side of their small, shaggy, but brave and hardy steeds, a small cask, or 'keg', as it was called, of illicit whisky, manufactured amid the wilds of Aberdeenshire or the glens of the Grampians. They took up a position on some commanding eminence during the day, where they could, as from a watch-tower, descry the distant approach of the enemy, the exciseman or gauger : then, when night fell, every man to horse, descending the mountains only six miles from Brechin, they scoured the plains, rattled into the villages and towns, disposing of their whisky to agents they had everywhere; and, now safe, returned at their leisure, or often in a triumphal procession. They were often caught, no doubt, with the contraband whisky in their possession. Then they were subjected to heavy fines besides the loss of their goods. But – daring, stout, active fellows – they often broke through the nets, and were not slack, if it offered them a chance of escape, to break the heads of the gaugers. I have seen a troop of thirty of them riding in Indian file, and in broad day, through the streets of Brechin, after they had succeeded in disposing of their whisky, and, as they rode leisurely along, beating time with their formidable codgels on the empty barrels to the great amusement of the public and mortification of the excisemen, who had nothing for it but to bite their nails and stand, as best they could, the raillery of the smugglers and the laughter of the people . . . Everybody, with a few exceptions, drank what was in reality illicit whisky – far superior to that made under the eye of the Excise – lord and lairds, members of Parliament and ministers of the Gospel, and everybody else.

Another Scottish minister, this time in the Borders, remembered whisky smuggling at the beginning of the nineteenth century. In his posthumous book entitled by its editors *Reminiscences of Yarrow* James Russell wrote:

About fifty years ago, smuggling was carried on to a considerable extent. It was generally counted a very slight offence to defraud the revenue in this form, and informers were not to be found. The recesses of the mountains afforded ready opportunities for the preparation of *mountain-dew*, and the old corn-mill supplying the materials, the part of the river at which it stood was appropriately termed the '*maut* pool'. The still was a very primitive affair, consisting generally of a hole dug in some quiet nook; the roof was formed by some strong branches covered with turf; and there was no outward indication of its whereabouts. The farmer was usually let into the secret, lest, in riding or coursing over his farm, he and his horses had come to grief.

But it was in the Highlands that illicit distilling was most common and where the battle of wits between distillers and excisemen waxed most furious – ending, in the great majority of cases, in victory for the former. The rugged nature of the country favoured the natives, who knew every inch of it, against the intruding excise officers. Even a reward of £5 offered by the Government to anyone reporting the whereabouts of an illicit still helped rather than hindered the illicit distillers. As Sir Robert Bruce Lockhart explained in his book *Scotch* :

In those days the most expensive part of a primitive still was the 'worm', a coiled copper pipe which condenses into liquid the hot vapour from the wash-still and then passes it into the spirit-still. When their copper-pipe was worn out, the smugglers used to dismantle their still, taking good care to remove whatever might be of further use to them, but leaving the worn-out worm and other minor implements to show that a still had been there. One of the smugglers would then go to the gauger, report that he had discovered a still, and receive the £5 as a reward. With the money thus acquired the smugglers would then buy the copper for a new pipe and set up their still in another glen.

These illicit distillers were not, of course, full-time; they were farmers who distilled their own whisky in the old Highland tradition of family distilling. From the very first confrontation between Government and Scotch whisky the governmental ambition was to transform whisky distilling from a private family affair to public manufacture by professionals. And with the passing of the Act of 1823 the completion of this process became inevitable.

The 1823 Act was a final attempt by the Government to solve a hitherto insoluble problem. In that year there were 14,000 official discoveries of illicit stills (which gives some idea of the number there must have been that were not detected). It seemed impossible to prevent Scotsmen, especially Highlanders, from distilling whisky privately in small stills wherever the geographical conditions were favourable. But complaints from the legal Lowland distillers about the unfair competition from smuggled Highland whisky produced frequent debates both in the Commons and the Lords on the question of whisky control and, after more than a century of constantly shifting and uniformly unsuccessful measures, it became increasingly felt that a completely new approach to the problem was called for. It was the intervention in the House of Lords of Alexander Gordon, fourth Duke of Gordon, that proved decisive. The Duke, 'the greatest subject in Britain' as a contemporary called him, was a great landowner in Inverness-shire and Banffshire (great whisky country). He argued that you could not stop the Highlander from distilling : he was a natural distiller and whisky was his traditional national drink. If, he maintained, legislation were passed that would provide realistic opportunities for the legal manufacture of whisky under reasonably favourable conditions and of as good quality as the product of illicit stills, he and his fellow landed proprietors in Scotland would do their best to suppress illicit distilling and smuggling and encourage their tenants to take out licences for their stills. Largely as a result of the Duke's promise, and after a commission under Thomas Wallace (later Lord Wallace), vice-president of the Board of Trade, had sat for two years, the 1823 Act was passed. This sanctioned the distilling of whisky on payment of duty of 2s 3d per gallon of proof spirit and a licence fee of £10 on all stills with a capacity of 40 gallons or over. Forty gallons (rather than the 500 gallons of the 1814 Act) now became the legal minimum size.

The effect of the new Act was not immediate, and illicit distilling went on, though in diminishing quantities, for some time. It was not, in fact, until the complete commercializing of whisky production and distribution by the blended whisky houses of the latter part of the nineteenth century that illicit distilling virtually disappeared. It did not completely disappear even then, and some illicit activity went on well into the twentieth century; but by then it had long ceased to be a real problem. The 14,000 detections in 1823 diminished to 692 in 1834, 177 in 1844, 73 in 1854, 19 in 1864 and 6 in 1874. There was a short-lived revival of illicit distilling after the repeal of the Malt Tax in 1880 made it safe for the illicit distiller to engage in all the processes except the final brewing and distilling, and the Depression of the early 1930s produced another temporary revival of illicit distilling. Steadily increasing taxation of whisky after the Second World War has prevented the total disappearance of the illicit still, and it seems fairly certain that a limited amount of illicit distilling is still going on.

It was not an easy job to persuade Highland farmers to take out licences and become legitimate distillers. But the example was set by George Smith of Glenlivet in 1824. Before then, like many others in that great whisky district, he had been distilling illicitly. There were in fact 200 illicit stills in Glenlivet in 1823. Smith, an unusually well educated farmer who had been trained as an architect, had his illicit still on his farm of Upper Drumin (farther up the hill from the present Glenlivet distillery). Encouraged by the Duke of Gordon, Smith rebuilt his distillery on a larger scale and took out a licence: thus in 1824 the Glenlivet distillery came legally into being, producing a great whisky which, still known as 'Smith's Glenlivet', is one of the very finest of Highland malt whiskies and indeed has a claim to be considered the champion of them all. Glenlivet had been producing excellent whisky long before this; but now the name 'Glenlivet' could be freely used and boasted about as the home of great whisky – so much so, indeed, that the word became synonymous in Scotland with good whisky. The old rhyme says:

> Glenlivet it has castles three,
> Drumin, Blairfindy and Deskie,
> And also one distillery
> More famous than the castles three.

One could fill a book with references to Glenlivet in literature, which became a legal whisky and remained legendary after it became legal. Witness the case of the valiant Macpherson of W. E. Aytoun's poem, who

> had a son
> Who married Noah's daughter;
> And nearly spoiled ta Flood,
> By trinking up ta water:
>
> Which he would have done,
> I at least pelieve it,
> Had ta mixture peen
> Only half Glenlivet.

Glenlivet had a reputation long before George Smith went legitimate. When George IV visited Scotland in 1822, two years before Smith's conversion, he insisted on having it. Elizabeth Grant of Rothiemurchus has a vivid account of what happened:

Lord Conyngham, the Chamberlain, was looking everywhere for pure Glenlivet whisky; the King drank nothing else. It was not to be had out of the Highlands. My father sent word to me – I was the cellarer – to empty my pet bin, where was whisky long in wood, long in uncorked bottles, mild as milk, and the true contraband *goût* in it. Much as I grudged this treasure it made our fortunes afterwards, showing on what trifles great events depend. The whisky, and fifty brace of ptarmigan all shot by one man, went up to Holyrood House, and were graciously received and made much of, and a reminder of this attention at a proper moment by the gentlemanly Chamberlain ensured to my father the Indian judgeship.

Earlier the King, on his arrival at Leith, had, in J. G. Lockhart's words, 'called for a bottle of Highland whisky, and having drunk his health in this national liquor, desired a glass to be filled for [Sir Walter Scott, who had welcomed him]. Sir Walter, after draining his own bumper, made a request that the King would condescend to bestow on him the glass out of which his Majesty had just drunk his health.' This is the glass that Scott, having put it into his pocket, forgot about when, on returning home, he found the poet Crabbe awaiting him; he sat down on it and it smashed to pieces, giving him a painful but insignificant scratch. There is no record of whether the Highland whisky consumed on that occasion was Glenlivet or not.

George Smith had to contend against much local opposition. Some of his neighbours, considering him the worst of blacklegs, threatened to burn down his new distillery — indeed, one distillery on Deeside was burned down in 1825. But Smith was undaunted, even though for some years he thought it prudent to go about with 'a pair of hair-trigger pistols' in his belt, presented to him by the laird of Aberlour. In 1825 and 1826 three more legal distilleries were started in Glenlivet, but had to give up in the face of opposition from the smugglers. But in the long run the 1823 Act did work, and steadily as the century advanced legitimate distilleries emerged in the Highlands. Smith himself reaped the reward of his pioneering in legitimacy: the subsequent history of the Glenlivet distillery is told in another chapter.

—— 3 ——
The Patent Still and its Consequences

In the last chapter I said something about the Stein family (who inter-married with the Haigs) and their large distillery at Kilbagie, Clackmannanshire. The owner of Kilbagie distillery in 1826 was Robert Stein, and it was in that year that he invented a process for the rapid distillation of grain whisky, a 'patent still' that represented quite a different method from the traditional pot-still method used in making malt whisky. Stein's method was quickly introduced by his cousin John Haig at his distillery at Cameron Bridge, Fife. But it was soon superseded by an improved patent still invented in 1830 by Aeneas Coffey, formerly inspector-general of Excise in Ireland. Both Stein and Coffey had carried out some of their experiments in developing their methods of distillation at the Islay distillery of Port Ellen, built in 1825 and in 1826 taken over by John Ramsay, Member of Parliament for Stirling and a prominent Glasgow business man with a great interest in the whisky trade. Known as the Coffey still or patent still, Aeneas Coffey's invention had obvious commercial advantages over the pot still : it can produce whisky more quickly, more cheaply, in much greater quantities and in a continuous process. Is is also independent of locality, in the sense that the quality of its product is not related to the local peat and water and other mysterious local factors which help to determine the individuality of the whisky produced at each pot-still malt distillery. The patent still was designed for the production of a whisky out of a mixture of malted and unmalted barley mashed with other cereals. Its product derived no peaty flavour from the malt, for the malt had not been dried over peat fires, nor did it contain the oils and aromatic substances that give malt whisky its characteristic flavour. As it is an improved design of Coffey's patent still that today produces that grain whisky with

66

which malt whiskies are blended to give the popular blended Scotch whiskies of our time, we had better take a look at how it works. The much debated question concerning the merits of patent-still grain whisky, and indeed the question whether it can properly be called Scotch whisky at all, will be an important part of the story later.

Scottish grain whisky today is made largely from maize with a small amount of malted barley (not dried over peat fires); unmalted barley is also sometimes used with the maize. The unmalted cereal is crushed and then cooked at a temperature of 140° C. to break up the starch before being blown off into a mash tun. Wet ground malted barley is now added (one-fifth of the amount of the unmalted cereal), then hot water, and the mixture is stirred. As with the making of malt whisky, the enzyme diastase of the malted barley converts the starch in the cereal into maltose, producing the liquid wort. The fermenting of the wort with yeast in wash-backs is done in much the same way as the fermenting of the wort in the making of malt whisky, with the same result. The wash is then pumped into the Coffey still, and henceforward the process is radically different from that employed in the making of pot-still malt whisky. The Coffey still consists of two linked copper columns, forty to fifty feet high; these are the analyser and the rectifier. Each is divided horizontally into chambers by perforated copper plates. Steam is led by a pipe into the analyser and proceeds up the analyser and then through the linking pipe into the rectifier. The wash which is all the time being pumped into the rectifier comes down the rectifier in a coiled copper pipe and then by the connecting wash pipe into the top of the analyser. It moves down, chamber by chamber, but not through the perforations (through which the steam ascends) as the rising steam prevents this so that the level of the wash rises until it reaches the entrance of the drip pipe, which is a little above the plate, and by the drip pipe descends to the lower chamber. The wash descends in this way compartment by compartment, and by the time it reaches the base of the analyser all the alcohol which it had contained has been vaporized by the steam. The alcohol vapour and the steam rise up through the analyser and go down the connecting vapour pipe (which emerges from the top of the analyser) into the rectifier. As the alcohol vapour and the steam move up the rectifier, chamber by chamber, the new incoming wash, coming down the rectifier in its winding pipe, cools them, so that condensation takes place.

The ingenuity of the process is illustrated by the fact that the vapours that heat the wash are also condensed by the wash. Another important point in the patent-still process is the progressive condensation of the alcohol vapour as it rises through the chambers of the rectifier. It is only the almost pure alcohol that gets to the top. The higher alcohols, esters and aldehydes distil first and drop out through a pipe at the bottom of the rectifier to be eventually returned to the analyser for re-distilling. Farther up the rectifier column, the residual alcohol vapour distils, producing 95 per cent ethyl alcohol and water, and this is drawn off through a cooling worm to the stainless-steel spirit receivers. Like pot-still whisky, it is then reduced in strength by the addition of water before being passed into barrels for maturing. Patent-still whisky, being nearer neutral spirits than pot-still malt whisky, takes less time to mature and changes less in maturing.

What exactly is the product of the Coffey or patent still? Dr Philip Schidrowitz, writing in the 1911 edition of the *Encyclopaedia Britannica*, hotly denied that the product was true 'silent' or 'neutral' spirits – i.e. alcohol and water. 'They possess a distinct flavour,' he wrote, 'which varies at different distilleries, and analysis discloses the fact that they contain very appreciable quantities of the "secondary" products which distinguish potable spirits from plain alcohol.' And Dr Schidrowitz (who was not altogether disinterested in the matter, as he was a member of the Council of the Institute of Brewing and had close contacts with both the brewing and distilling industries) went on to say that as a result of 'an extensive investigation of the question' carried out by himself, it had been shown 'that the relative proportion of "secondary" products in Highland Malt, Lowland

Malt and "grain" whiskies respectively, is as 3 : 2 : 1'. The informative pamphlet put out by the Distillers Company Limited (DCL) in 1962 – and, as we shall see, DCL became early in the present century a tremendous force in popularizing blends of malt and grain whiskies as the standard Scotch whisky so that their view, also, can hardly be considered disinterested – calls patent-still grain whisky 'still a true Scotch whisky, but lighter in body than the malt whisky of the pot-still'. On the other hand, Neil Gunn, that great champion of pot-still malt whisky, in his stimulating if idiosyncratic book *Whisky and Scotland*, published in 1935, wrote : 'The product of the pot still contains the oils and aromatic substances that gives true whisky its body and flavour. The product of the patent still is almost pure alcohol, flavourless, and is mainly used for industrial and scientific purposes.' Bruce Lockhart expresses a more moderate view : 'Grain whisky is lighter in weight and less distinctive in taste than malt whisky. It does not improve in cask in the same manner or to anything like the same extent as malt whisky, but it is wrong to describe it as a neutral spirit.'

As we shall see, the future of patent-still grain whisky was to lie chiefly in blended Scotch whisky; its chief use today is as it has been for many years to 'lighten' the heavier malt whiskies with which it is blended. The relative merits of these blends and of single malt whiskies will be discussed in due course; all that need be said here is that it is on its merits as a blending agent that patent-still grain whisky must stand or fall. It is very rarely drunk now unblended, although it once was. Today the only available patent-still grain whisky in bottle is *Choice Old Cameron Brig*, made at Cameronbridge Distillery by Scottish Grain Distillers Ltd. and bottled and sold by John Haig & Co. Ltd. It is sold locally, where I am told it is preferred by the natives to a blended whisky. The only place in England where I have found it on sale is the Fosseway Restaurant and Hotel, Newark-on-Trent, where they have a remarkable range of Scotch whiskies on sale in the bar, including a wide range of malts. I find it clear and sharp in taste, almost antiseptic indeed, with nothing at all of what I would call whisky character. The only other grain whisky I have drunk by itself is North British, a seven-year-old sample of which was made available to me by courtesy of an Edinburgh blending firm. This has a sharp, pungent, acidy smell ('like surgical spirit', my wife remarked as I passed the glass to her, and she sniffed it). Its sharpness caught me at the back of the throat as I drank. It seemed to have little or no body, but all surface flavour, and that flavour of a pungent sweet sharpness that makes one think more of a chemistry laboratory than a bar. My own experience with patent-still grain whisky, then, suggests that while it has a part to play in blends it is not a whisky to drink by itself, nor can it begin to compare as a drink with a pot-still malt whisky. But it is clearly not just 'silent spirit' : indeed, it is rather noisy.

The arrival of the Coffey still produced no immediate revolution. Its use was legalized by Treasury warrant in September 1832 but it was not until 1839 that the Board of Excise issued the appropriate instructions to the Excise Officers who would have to supervise its working. There was no question yet of producing blends of Lowland grain and Highland malt whiskies for the English market. Scotch whisky – whether malt or grain – which was sent to England was not as a rule drunk as whisky; it was rectified and turned into gin. The Royal Commission which sat from 1833 to 1836 under Sir Henry Brooke Parnell (later Lord Congleton, the distinguished Whig economist and financial expert), one of many such commissions enquiring into the question of potable spirits in Britain, observed that in England there was 'scarcely any demand for whisky in the pure state in which it is prepared for consumption in Scotland and Ireland'. The Commission also put its finger on one factor that was hindering the export of Scotch whisky to England : 'There is no doubt that orders for the fine quality of malt whisky from the Highlands would be increased to a great extent both for the use of private families in England and also for ship stores, if spirits were permitted to be shipped in casks of smaller capacity than eighty gallons.' They went so far as to suggest that 'an arrangement might be made under which the exportation of Scotch spirits in bottles might be permitted in the same way as is practised with regard to foreign wines'. It was not in fact until Gladstone's Spirits Act of 1860 that this aspect of the Parnell Report was implemented and whisky was allowed to be imported from Scotland to England in bottles.

The 1823 Act, as we have seen, had an immediately beneficial effect in encouraging the development of good legal distillers of pot-still malt whisky and in lessening illicit distilling and smuggling. But further legislation and competition between grain and malt distillers changed the picture within a decade. In 1822, just before the new policy was introduced, something over two million gallons of tax-paid Scotch whisky were recorded as having been consumed; in 1825 – the year of an important Consolidating Act which ironed out most discrepancies in the manufacture and sale of spirits in different parts of the United Kingdom – the figure was almost six million. Encouraged by this, the Government thought the time ripe to increase taxation. In 1826 they raised the tax from 2s 4d to 2s 10d per imperial gallon (the imperial gallon was now the legal measure for spirit duties in Scotland) and in 1830 to 3s 4d. The result might have been predicted : legal consumption dropped again, and illicit distilling and smuggling rose. Government measures for prevention and detection stiffened. At the same time distillers, facing increasing competition, could not afford to let their whisky mature but for the most part sold it new. There was as yet no legislation governing the maturing of spirits. Distillers tried to solve their problems by building up exports, and slowly a small export trade was built up, chiefly from Glasgow. John Ramsay's distillery at Port Ellen, Islay, pioneered direct whisky export to the United States. From 1500 gallons of malt whisky exported from Scotland (excluding what went to England) in 1824, the figure rose to 25,000 gallons in 1834. A tiny trickle when compared with the massive exports of a later age, but still a pointer to the future.

An act of 1848 allowed English distillers to use a great

variety of raw materials (including molasses and treacle) for purposes of distilling, but the Scots were still restricted to grain, and the Scottish Lowland patent-still distiller felt that he was unfairly treated compared with his English rival. These distillers then turned to a new solution : if competition was making it difficult for them, they would try combination. The first movement in this direction came in 1856, when six of the leading Scottish patent-still distillers entered into a trade agreement, sharing the trade among themselves in fixed proportions in order to avoid over-production and its resulting slumps. The arrangement did not last and nine years later a similar association was formed. Arrangements were discussed with Irish and English distillers and much ebb and flow of proposals and counter-proposals went on among interested parties in all three countries. Finally, in 1875 it was proposed 'that the principal firms engaged in the grain distillery business should form themselves into one company under the Limited Liabilities Act'. In April 1877 six Lowland grain patent-still distillers combined to form the Distillers Company Limited with a nominal capital of two million pounds and headquarters in Edinburgh. The firms were : M. Macfarlane & Co., Port Dundas Distillery, Glasgow; John Bald & Co., Carsebridge Distillery, Alloa; John Haig and Co., Cameron Bridge Distillery, Fife; McNab Bros. & Co., Glenochil Distillery, Menstrie; Robert Mowbray, Cambus Distillery, Alloa; Stewart & Co., Kirkliston Distillery, West Lothian. These were all Lowland firms. By now the cities of Scotland – Leith (which had become the whisky capital), Edinburgh, Perth, Glasgow, Aberdeen – had become the centre of the whisky trade. And Andrew Usher & Co. of Edinburgh, who were agents for Glenlivet first for the South of Scotland and England and from 1864 for the world, had already pioneered the blending of pot-still malt and patent-still grain whiskies. One other factor was necessary to achieve the great break-through of Scotch whisky and make it a standard drink in England and throughout the world. This was a stimulus to turn people away from brandy as the fashionable English drink in favour of Scotch. It was an event across the Channel that achieved this.

Between 1858 and 1863 there was a great deal of importation into France of American vines for grafting purposes. (The native American vine east of the Rocky Mountains is very hardy, and its roots are resistant to the *Phylloxera vastatrix*, an insect which destroys growing vines by attacking their roots and leaves. The European vine, *Vitis vinifera*, which grows also in California but not east of the Rockies, is vulnerable to phylloxera.) It was the imported American plants that brought the deadly insect which invaded Europe and devastated French vineyards. It was first observed in France in 1865, and after that French wine production fell steadily year by year until the middle eighties. In the end many French vineyards had to be replanted entirely with French vines grafted on to eastern American phylloxera-resistant stocks. In the 1880s the vineyards of the Grande Champagne, the centre of the Cognac district, were terribly devastated and the production of cognac brought almost to a standstill. One of the expedients resorted to by the cognac producers in this crisis was to blend a very little cognac with other spirits made from a variety of raw materials. In the 1890s it was impossible to refill cognac stocks, and the British brandy drinker had to look elsewhere for a comparable spirit. (At least one notable port was in 1897 fortified with Scotch whisky instead of the normal brandy.) By now blends of pot-still malt and patent-still grain Scotch whisky were being vigorously marketed in England by energetic and enterprising Scottish whisky firms. It was the combination of the results of phylloxera in France, the development of blends of malt and grain whiskies in Scotland, and energetic commercial activity and brilliant salesmanship, that put blended Scotch whisky on the sideboard of the English gentleman at the end of the nineteenth century. Winston Churchill once recalled that 'my father could never have drunk whisky except when shooting on a moor or in some very dull chilly place. He lived in the age of brandy and soda.' Whisky and soda[16] began to replace brandy and soda as the Englishman's drink later in the century; and as it would be criminal to add soda to a fine Highland malt whisky, it was the blending of malt with grain that made whisky and soda, like the American highball (which includes a great deal of soda and ice), a rational potation.

The blending of cognac with other spirits, resulting from the shortage of cognac caused by the ravages of phylloxera in French vineyards, was symptomatic of the general movement towards blending in the latter part of the nineteenth century. At the same time, concern was being shown in government quarters about the adulteration of potable spirits. A Licensing Act of 1872 had prohibited adulteration, but the relevant section was repealed in the 1874 Licensing Act. However, Disraeli's great Sale of Food and Drugs Act of 1875, the first truly comprehensive legislation on the subject and the principal statute until 1928, forbade ingredients which would 'render the article injurious to health', and in 1879 an amending Act took special note of the adulteration of spirits. It was under this legislation that the right of patent-still grain whisky and of blends of this with malt whisky to call themselves Scotch whisky was challenged in the new century.

Meanwhile, blended Scotch whisky flourished and the great whisky boom was on. In 1892 there were 130 working distilleries in Scotland; in 1898 there were 161; new ones were built and old ones expanded. DCL, in a pamphlet of 1905,[17] congratulated itself on what had happened. 'Previous to this [the blending of grain and malt whiskies] the principal whisky drinkers were confined to Scotland and Ireland. In England, wines and brandies occupied important positions as fashionable beverages. Such whisky as was consumed was largely the product of the Irish pot still, which consisted, as it does still, of a mash of from 30 to 50 per cent of malt and the remainder of unmalted wheat, rye, oats, etc. The pure Scotch malt whisky was even then admittedly too heavy for the ordinary palate, but, with the advent of the Scotch blend, being an admixture of the finest Highland malt whisky with a pure grain whisky (which latter the Scotch patent-still had now brought to a state of high perfection), the public taste all over England underwent a complete change. Irish whiskey gradually lost favour, brandy and wines went out of fashion, and, led by the medical profession, the consumption of Scotch blended whiskies soon took a leading place.' DCL – which we must remember was originally an association of grain-whisky distillers who had only recently enlarged their activities by going into blending and malt-whisky distilling – had every right to be pleased. Fifteen years earlier a Select Committee of the House of Commons, looking into certain questions relating to both domestic and foreign spirits, had remarked in their report : 'They gave evidence that there was increased demand for Whisky of a milder kind and the blends of pot still and patent still Whisky were in large demand by the consumers, which thus obtained a cheaper and milder Whisky containing a smaller quantity of fusel oil and other by-products.'

Of course, these 'other by-products' were what gave pot-still malt whisky its characteristic flavour and quality. And, of course, 'mildness' is a matter of maturing the whisky properly and of reducing the proof with water. And, again of course, if the brilliant salesmanship which went into the marketing of blended Scotch whisky in England in the second half of the nineteenth century had been put at the service of the marketing of matured malt whisky instead, it might have had the same success. I confess that I am always a bit dubious about arguments from the popular palate when, in the first place, brilliant and intensive advertising and merchandising have largely created that palate and, in the second place, my own observation has demonstrated that most whisky-and-soda drinkers, even if they religiously ask for the same brand each time, do not in fact notice if they are given something different. Indeed, I doubt whether a genuinely discriminating popular palate for something like whisky exists or ever has existed among whisky-and-soda drinkers, and I do not think that this doubt is answered by the indisputable fact that people do have their favourite brands and that some brands are more popular in some parts of the world than others. It is a question of advertising and habit. This is not to say that many blended Scotch whiskies are not admirable drinks of their kind; they are indeed, and they will be discussed in a later chapter.

So I read the report of the Select Committee of 1890–1 a little sceptically when it goes on to say: 'It is stated that public taste requires a Whisky of less marked characteristics than formerly, and to gratify this desire various blends are made, either by the mixture of pot still products, or by the addition of silent spirits from the patent still [it is interesting that patent-still whisky is here regarded simply as "silent spirits"]. In the latter case cheapness is often the purpose of the blend, but it is also stated that it incorporates the mixture of several Whiskies more efficiently.' The report did note, however, that the blends were often made 'of old spirits of various kinds' and even that these were 'frequently kept in bond for a considerable time', thus emphasizing one important virtue of the more responsible whisky blenders: they offered the public a mature spirit, not something straight from the still. Nevertheless, there was as yet no legislation compelling whisky producers to mature the whisky for a minimum period before selling it: this had to wait until 1915, and even then the compulsory period was only three years. The Select Committee of 1890–1, however, concluded 'from the evidence submitted to us, that the compulsory bonding of all spirits for a certain period is unnecessary and would harass trade'. The public, they said, 'show a marked preference for old spirits' and therefore 'it is not desirable to pass any compulsory law in regard to age, especially as the general feeling of the Trade is that such an obligation would harass commerce, and be an unfair burden on particular classes of spirits'.

The triumph of Scotch whisky in England in the latter half of the nineteenth century was not entirely the result of the three factors I have already discussed. There was a fourth, less tangible, factor which certainly must have had something to do with it. This was the development of a *mystique* about Scotland which really began with the publication of Walter Scott's narrative poem *The Lady of the Lake* in 1810. The romantic descriptions of Highland scenery in this enormously popular poem, while not the first admiring descriptions of such scenery, were certainly the first to be circulated on such a large scale and have such a remarkable effect. For Scott virtually invented the Highlands as a holiday area for English tourists, and in the wake of this tourism there developed a spate of what modern critics have disparagingly called 'tartanry'. When Queen Victoria built Balmoral Castle on Deeside, Aberdeenshire, in the early 1850s, the seal of royal approval was set on the enthusiasm for things Scottish. There was a revival of the wearing of the kilt. Scottish souvenirs, from tartan tea-cosies to miniature bagpipes, found their way to the tea-tables and chimney-pieces of English visitors. And, of course, any Englishman of wealth and standing had to do some shooting in Scotland in the autumn and preferably also to own a shooting lodge or a house in Scotland. In Oscar Wilde's play, *The Importance of Being Earnest*, the late Mr Thomas Cardew had three addresses : '149 Belgrave Square, SW; Gervase Park, Dorking, Surrey; and the Sporran, Fifeshire, NB'. (NB=North Britain, i.e. Scotland). It was his possession of a Scottish house that put the seal on his respectability and social standing. (It would not, in fact, have been likely to be in Fife but in the Highlands.)

The image of the Scots as picturesque, romantic, noble, even primitive, goes back to Macpherson's *Ossian* of 1760, but it was only in the second half of the nineteenth century that this image became blended with a passion for tourism, the manufacture of souvenirs, and a widespread, popular desire to imitate the habits of the gentry. There was a great deal of vulgarity about this conception of Scotland, and a great deal of condescension too. It was oddly mixed with music-hall notions of the Scots as a nation of hairy-kneed, kilt-wearing consumers of whisky and haggis who sang songs about a wee hoose amang the heather. Harry Lauder was the apotheosis of this conception of Scotland. It is a view which has been violently repudiated by thoughtful Scotsmen today, who see this concept of the Scot very much as the modern Negro sees the old-fashioned picture of the happy and comic Negro of popular entertainment some fifty years and less ago. Nevertheless, it was bound up with the fashion for things Scottish which helped in the popularization of Scotch whisky in England.

The story of the great whisky blenders and merchants who made 'Scotch' a household word in England and across the seas is told in the next chapter. But in addition to the 'big five' – Haig, Dewar, Buchanan, Walker and Mackie – and other great names which have survived up to our own day, there were others who tried unsuccessfully to take advantage of the whisky boom. The most notorious failure, and one which illustrates very clearly the nature of the whisky boom, was that of Pattison's who started with a wholesale grocery firm in Leith and in the early eighties expanded into whisky blending in the hope of a quick fortune. At first the firm, which called itself Pattison, Elder and Co. and then became a limited liability company calling itself simply Pattison's Ltd., had immense success, and Robert and Walter Pattison, the two brothers who controlled it, made or appeared to have made an enormous amount of money. They built themselves a palatial house in Leith Walk, Edinburgh, and lived there in conspicuous extravagance. Robert Pattison also bought a country estate near Peebles, and it is said that on returning from it to Edinburgh he used to deliberately let himself miss the train so that he could order a private train at the cost of £5 1s 0d per mile. They splashed their advertising about with enormous gusto, on one occasion releasing hundreds of grey parrots trained to cry, 'Drink Pattison's whisky!' The public, eager to participate in the Pattison fortune, invested heavily in Pattison's Ltd. The firm itself got ample credits from the Scottish banks. More and more distilleries were built, whisky production went up and up. The public invested more and more. But soon it became clear that production had far outstripped demand. The Pattisons ran into trouble and after desperate but unsuccessful attempts to get further finance in order to reorganize and re-float the company it suspended payment on 6 December 1898, with effects that reverberated through the whole whisky trade. Investors and speculators hoping for quick and easy money lost all; distilleries lost money and some had to close down; other firms were involved and seriously distressed. The Pattison brothers were tried for fraud and sentenced to imprisonment, Robert, the elder and the leading spirit, to eighteen months and Walter to eight months. Among other things, the Pattison failure demonstrated the dangers of over-production and encouraged DCL in its policy of amalgamation.

But the greatest storm of all that the booming Scotch whisky trade had to weather was the result of legal doubt as to whether blended Scotch whisky was really whisky at all. In 1904 the Borough Council of Islington had successfully brought proceedings under the Food and Drugs Act against certain public houses for offering for sale brandy (which, as we have seen, was now liable to be a blend of cognac and other spirits as a result of the devastation wrought by phylloxera) which was 'not of the nature, substance and quality of the article demanded by the purchaser'. The following year was the turn of whisky. In November 1905 summonses were taken out as test cases by the Islington Borough Council against certain publicans who were charged with selling as whisky a spirit 'not of the nature, substance and quality demanded' by a purchaser who asked for whisky. Mr Fordham, the magistrate of the North London Police Court before whom the case was heard, gave judgement against the defendants, which meant that patent-still whisky was not true whisky and that blends containing it represented adulteration in terms of the Food and Drugs Act. The decision was an immense shock to DCL and the Scotch blended-whisky industry in general. The grain distillers encouraged the defendants to appeal, which they did. The appeal was lodged to Quarter Sessions, and in May and June 1906 Mr W. R. McConnell, KC, sitting with a bench of lay magistrates, heard the case. After seven sittings, it became apparent that the bench was equally divided, so that no decision was possible. So the earlier judgement stood : the grain distillers were despondent and the malt distillers jubilant. The grain distillers and blenders clearly could not let matters rest there, and after discussions it was decided that DCL should ask the President of the Board of Trade to appoint a Committee or a Royal Commission to settle the 'what is whisky?' question (as it came to be called) once and for all. The Islington Borough Council were also anxious to have an authoritative ruling on the matter, and they too approached the President of the Board of Trade. He was John Burns, the labour leader and first artisan to reach cabinet rank, no friend to the whisky trade, for he knew at first-hand the effects of drinking cheap liquor in the slums of big cities. But the joint representations of DCL and the Islington Borough Council eventually had their effect and in July 1907 Parliament agreed to Mr Burns's request for a Royal Commission, which was set up in February 1908 under Lord James of Hereford, the distinguished Liberal lawyer, statesman and cricket enthusiast. Its terms of reference were to enquire into 'Whisky and Other Potable Spirits' with a view to determining, in the interests of consumers and of public health in general, whether restrictions should be placed on the materials or processes by means of which spirit called whisky could be manufactured in the United Kingdom, and whether a minimum period should be fixed for maturing whisky in bond.

Although the Commission included six scientific and medical experts, they all seemed to have started from scratch so far as their knowledge of whisky was concerned. They tried to learn. Revenue officials visited thirty-nine public houses in England and twenty-three in Scotland and asked for 'a glass of whisky': what they received in answer to this request they took away and analysed. In every case it was patent-still grain whisky. An important question was whether consumers who asked for whisky and received patent-still spirit knew in advance exactly what it was that they would get and in fact expected and wanted to get it. The Commission decided that they did. In an interim report issued in June 1908 the Commission recommended 'that no restriction should be placed upon the processes of, or apparatus used in, the distillation of any spirit to which the term "whiskey" may be applied as a trade description'.

They further recommended 'that the term "whiskey" having been recognized in the past as applicable to a potable spirit manufactured from (1) malt, or (2) malt and unmalted barley or other cereals should not be denied to the product manufactured from such materials'. (Note that the Commission consistently spelt 'whisky' with an 'e' – 'whiskey' – a spelling then regular in official Government publications on whisky but now confined to Irish and American whiskey.)

The Commission's final report was published on 28 July 1909. It had held thirty-seven sittings for the purpose of taking evidence, examined 116 witnesses, and considered various documents submitted to it. Several members of the Commission had visited distilleries in Scotland and Ireland and even some brandy distilleries and warehouses in France. They had looked into the history of whisky-drinking in Britain and in particular the development of blending. 'Blending for the English and foreign markets on a large scale,' the report states in its historical survey, 'seems to have commenced between 30 and 40 years ago. Since that time the practice has gone on increasing. It has undoubtedly done very much to popularize Scotch whiskey.' They go on to point out that 'it would probably be safe to say that the majority of Englishmen who drink whiskey seldom drink anything but a blend'. They seem to have been much influenced by the popularity of blends in England and by the fact that almost two-thirds of the whisky then being distilled in Scotland was patent-still whisky. There is no evidence that the members of the Commission had themselves done any comparative tasting of different pot-still malt whiskies and patent-still whisky : they depended on analysis. 'On reference to the analyses, it will be seen that there is a very wide variation between whiskies from different distilleries; and that there is a very wide variation between whiskies from the same distilleries in different years.' As for the difference between pot-still and patent-still whisky, 'we have received no evidence to show that the form of the still has any necessary relation to the wholesomeness of the spirit produced'. And therefore 'we are unable to recommend that the use of the word "whiskey" should be restricted to spirit manufactured by the pot-still process'.

That was it. It was a glorious victory for the grain distillers and a defeat for the pot-still malt distillers. The report's 'general conclusion' was equally significant:

Our general conclusion, therefore, on this part of our inquiry is that 'whiskey' is a spirit obtained by distillation from a mash of cereal grains saccharified [i.e. turned into sugar] by the diastase of malt; that 'Scotch whiskey' is whiskey, as above defined, distilled in Scotland; and that 'Irish whiskey' is whiskey, as above defined, distilled in Ireland.

The report also refused to recommend that a declaration of the raw materials used in the preparation of whisky should be required, on the grounds that such a declaration interfered with trade and such interference could only be justified 'for the purpose of defeating fraud or semi-fraud, or to protect public health, or to prevent injurious adulteration'. They had found no evidence of fraud or injurious adulteration (note that the Commission throughout considered the 'wholesomeness' but not the taste and flavour of whisky) and gave it as their opinion that 'in the numerous distilleries existing in the United Kingdom the trade in whiskey seems to be honestly and fairly conducted'. The Commission stress on 'wholesomeness' is further evidenced in their conclusions concerning compulsory ageing. 'If compulsory bonding is considered as a means of securing the maturity and flavour, as distinct from the wholesomeness, of spirits, it must be borne in mind that spirits of different character do not mature with equal rapidity.' They were perfectly aware that 'a very much longer period is required for the maturation of a heavy pot-still malt whiskey, for example, than for a light patent-still whiskey' and that 'even in the case of spirits of the same character, differences in the condition of storage, such as the nature and size of the vessel in which the spirit is kept, the relative humidity of the place in which it is stored and climatic conditions generally, have a considerable effect in determining the rapidity of maturation'. They concluded that 'whatever period might be fixed would inevitably be open to one or two objections; it would either impose an unnecessary burden on particular classes of spirits, or it would be too short for the maturing of other classes'. Because, then, different kinds of whisky required different times to mature and the maturation rate in any case was affected by the size of the cask and by humidity and 'climatic conditions' generally, the Commission somewhat illogically concluded that no minimum period of any sort should be required. 'For the above reasons,' this section of the report concludes, 'we have come to the conclusion that it is not desirable to require a minimum period during which spirits should be matured in bond.'

It is important to note the definition of whisky given by the Commission : 'a spirit obtained by distillation from a mash of cereal grains saccharified by the diastase of malt'. As the description of the patent-still process at the beginning of this chapter makes clear, this definition will apply to patent-still grain whisky since a proportion of malted barley is always added in order to convert the starch in the cereal into maltose by means of the enzyme diastase. Patent-still grain whisky is thus clearly obtained 'from a mash of cereal grains saccharified by the diastase of malt'. So, of course, is pot-still malt whisky, though there the cereal used is always barley and all the barley is malted before mashing. Under this definition – which was reaffirmed in the Customs and Excise Act of 1952, though with the addition of the provision, first introduced in 1915, that it should be in a bonded warehouse in casks for at least three years – pot-still malt whisky, patent-still grain whisky, and blends of both, are all legally entitled to the appellation of 'Scotch whisky' if they are distilled in Scotland and have matured in bond for three years.

DCL, which had led the fight for the recognition of patent-still whisky and paid the grain distillers' costs, had triumphed gloriously. While the Commission was sitting DCL had advertised its Cambus whisky (a patent-still grain whisky made, as it still is, in the Cambus distillery, Alloa) in the *Daily Mail*, thus deliberately challenging the Islington decision and anticipating the Commission's report. The advertisement stressed the lightness and palatability of this whisky and its greater suitability for sedentary city-dwellers.[18] When the Commission's final report was issued, the advertisement disappeared. Since then Cambus has been used (so far as I know) only in blending.

This was not, of course, the end for the malt distillers, for pot-still malt whisky was and is an important ingredient of blended Scotch whisky. But it accelerated the decline of single malt whiskies and of 'vatted' malt whiskies (i.e. single malts of different ages and of different dates, though from the same pot-still distillery, blended together) as a drink readily available to the public, for the great majority of malt whiskies more and more went for blending. And it finally absolved the blenders from any obligation to state on the label of the whisky bottle what proportions of malt and grain were used. The blenders have never done this, and have indeed made a terrific mystery of their blending procedures. Writing in 1935 Neil Gunn complained that 'at the present time our most famous blends are mixtures of pot and patent still spirits in proportions which we do not know, but in which the preponderance is believed to be heavily patent'. He added : 'Yet the blender could very easily tell us what surely we have a right to know by stating on his label the proportions of patent and pot still and their respective ages. Nothing could be simpler. All reputable vineyards carry their vineyard and their year.' He went on, more belligerently still : 'A fine pot-still whisky is as noble a product of Scotland as any burgundy or champagne is of France. Patent-still spirit is no more a true whisky than, at the opposite extreme, is any of those cheap juices of the grape heavily fortified by raw spirit which we import from ends of the earth a true wine.'

The subject of patent-still whisky has always generated a certain amount of heat among dedicated malt-whisky drinkers, as well as among certain independent malt-whisky distillers. Shortly after the Royal Commission reported,

Colonel George Smith Grant, proprietor of the Glenlivet distillery (he was a nephew of John Gordon Smith who had succeeded his father George Smith, founder of the distillery), was presented with his portrait at a large gathering of friends. In the course of the speech he delivered in making the presentation, the Duke of Richmond and Gordon expressed the feelings of his audience on the Commission's report:

Quite recently a public enquiry has taken upon itself to decide – What is whisky? [*laughter*] And I regret to say that apparently anything that is made in Scotland, whatever its combination, is to be called Scots whisky. But for my part, I should prefer, and I think most of those whom I am addressing now would prefer, to trust to their own palates [*laughter*] rather than to the dogma of chemists, and to be satisfied with the whisky that is produced in Glenlivet ['*Hear, hear!*'] as against any other quality that is produced in Scotland.

DCL, however, continued to flourish. Its first years had not been easy. It was not until 1883 that it obtained a quotation on the Stock Exchange of Edinburgh and Glasgow, while the London Stock Exchange, to which it had applied for a quotation in January 1884, did not grant it until October 1886. Afraid of a DCL monopoly, a group of independent whisky merchants and blenders set up their own patent-still distillery in Gorgie, Edinburgh, in 1885, forming for the purpose the North British Distillery Company with William Sanderson as managing director and Andrew Usher as chairman. But this competition did not seriously bother DCL. In 1889 Mr William H. Ross became company secretary of DCL and gave it immense new impetus. It was after Ross became its chief executive that DCL became the largest producer of yeast in Britain (and, for that matter, in Europe). It was Ross, too, ever mindful of the larger interests of whisky production and distribution as a whole and of the need to stabilize prices and prevent wasteful competition, who pioneered the policy of amalgamation which eventually brought the 'Big Five' into DCL.

Lloyd George's budget of 29 April 1909, raising the duty on Scotch whisky from 11s per proof gallon to 14s 9d, was a blow to grain and malt distillers alike. At the same time growing American exports of blended Scotch whisky were threatened by the commission appointed by President Theodore Roosevelt to determine the proper legal definition of whisky. Its report was favourable to the blenders, but President Roosevelt would not accept it. In 1910, however, President Taft, who had succeeded Roosevelt in 1909, took with grand simplicity the decision that spirit made from cereals was whisky and spirit made from molasses was rum and that was that. He did, however, insist on proper labelling to distinguish a 'straight' whisky from a blend. It was to face the problems arising from Roosevelt's commission that the Scotch whisky exporters formed themselves into a Scottish Whisky Exporters' Association.

In spite of setbacks, and in spite of the 1909 budget, the Scotch whisky trade was flourishing in the years immediately preceding the First World War. DCL acquired its own patent-still distilleries in England and Ireland, and moved into the English gin and industrial alcohol trade. The lesson of the Pattison failure had been learned, especially by DCL, who substituted amalgamation, controlled acquisition, and controlled sales and prices for the runaway overproduction indulged in by rasher spirits in the height of the whisky boom. And the great whisky magnates who made blended Scotch whisky the popular international drink it still is today continued to expand their activities in both the home market and abroad. To these magnates I now turn.

——— 4 ———
Growth of the Big Five

One of the many paradoxes with which the history of
whisky is involved is that while Scotch whisky came down
to the Lowlands from the Highlands, its true home, the
oldest name in Scotch whisky is not Highland at all. It is
Haig (earlier del Hage, de Haga, de la Hage), a name of
Norman origin. A Norman knight of that name crossed the
Channel into England in the eleventh century and soon
afterwards the Haigs pushed north into Lowland Scotland,
where we find them well settled by the middle of the
thirteenth century. They built a Border castle at Bemersyde,
Berwickshire, and the Haigs of Bemersyde have been known
in Scottish history since Thomas of Erceldoune (modern
Earlston, near Bemersyde), the almost legendary thirteenth-
century seer and poet otherwise known as Thomas the
Rhymer, prophesied :

> Tide what may, whate'er betide,
> Haig shall be Haig of Bemersyde.

He has been proved right so far. But old Thomas said
nothing about Haig and whisky, which showed a certain
lack of prophetic power. For though a Haig fought at the
Battle of Stirling Bridge with William Wallace and another
was killed with his King at the Battle of Flodden – and
though in a later age a Haig was commander-in-chief of the
British forces in France and Flanders in the First World
War – the first association of the name today all over the
world is with Scotch whisky.

Like most Scottish Border families, the Haigs led a
turbulent life in the Middle Ages and well into the seventeenth century. Family feuding in the seventeenth century
brought Robert Haig, a Haig younger son, to leave the
family home and settle as a tenant farmer at Throsk, in

the parish of St Ninian's, Stirlingshire. Like many Scottish farmers of that and the next century, he carried on a certain amount of distilling on his farm. The following extract from volume I of the Session Record of St Ninian's Parish Church tells its own story :

Januar 4, 1665. – Compeared Robert Haig being summoned for Sabbath breaking and Wm. Reid, John Croby, William Harley and Christian Eason, Witnesses. Robert Haig denied he knew any such thing as was laid to his chairge. The witnesses deponed unanimously that they saw the caldron on the fyre, and a stand reiking and that they heard the goodwife say, 'the lasse has put on the caldron and played some after-wort' and she knew not whether her caldron was befor on the fyre on a Sabbath day and had she been at home it should not have been done (for she was byt presentlie cam'd from Alloway Church). So it being only some pynts· of small drink played by a servant lass naither maister nor maistresse accessarie to it upon engadgment of Christian carriage for the future, rebuked befor the Session.

This brush with the Kirk Session was obviously not serious, but it is fortunate for us that it occurred, for it gives us a glimpse into domestic distilling in the Scottish Lowlands in the seventeenth century. The Haigs continued to farm in Stirlingshire and neighbouring Clackmannanshire. They seem to have kept on distilling, too, for we find the name of Robert Haig's son Alexander in the Inland Revenue Collectors' accounts for 1699–1700 as having distilled 128 gallons six pints between 1 March and 1 June 1699. The spirit distilled was probably not a pure malt whisky : members of the Haig family had been in Holland in the seventeenth century and learned Dutch methods of distilling. Their distilling skill had not therefore come south from the Highlands. Nor had that of the Stein family (presumably of Dutch origin) who established the distilleries of Kilbagie and Kennetpans in Clackmannanshire early in the century. In 1751 John Haig, great-great-grandson of

Robert Haig of St Ninian's, married Margaret Stein, daughter of John Stein. When John Haig died at the age of fifty-three in 1773, Margaret's five fatherless sons were taken in as apprentices at their maternal grandfather's distillery of Kilbagie and there learned the art of distilling. Four of the five eventually founded their own distilleries elsewhere; but Andrew remained in Clackmannanshire and went into partnership at Kincardine with a member of what was to become the famous Irish distilling family of Jameson. It was the eldest son James who became the leading Lowland distiller after his grandfather's death. He developed the Edinburgh distilleries of Canonmills, Lochrin and Sunbury. John, after having been in partnership with James at Lochrin, established his own distillery at Bonnington, Leith. Robert went to Ireland and developed Dodderbank distillery, near Dublin. William, the youngest, settled in Fife and thus was the first to establish the long Haig connection, still existing, with that county. He built a distillery at Seggie, near St Andrews. Their sisters also did their bit for whisky. One married John Jameson who settled in Ireland and founded the firm of John Jameson and Son at Bow Street distillery, Dublin, in 1780, and another married John Philp, who had a distillery at Dolls, Menstrie, Clackmannanshire.

I mentioned in an earlier chapter the riots that broke out in June 1784 when a mob, believing that James Haig was using oats and potatoes in his Canonmills distillery, organized an attack on it, to which Haig replied by announcing that his distillery used only 'barley, rye, and sometimes such parcels of wheat as happen to receive damage, or are in quality unfit for bread'; this is pretty conclusive evidence that Haig used a mash of mixed cereals rather than malted barley in making his spirit. In this same statement Haig called attention to the fact that, far from consuming roots that would otherwise be available for cattle-feed, the distillery provides for cattle 'the grains or draff, and by that food alone they are fattened for the market'. The mob seem to have been placated, but James Haig continued to have his troubles, chiefly the tax problems that have already been discussed and competition from illicit distilling and smuggling, activities which were not confined to the Highlands. In 1777 400 illicit stills were said to have been discovered in the city of Edinburgh alone, compared with eight legal stills. In 1815 a most ingeniously contrived illicit still was discovered under the arch of the South Bridge, Edinburgh.

James Haig continued throughout his life to be a chief spokesman before the Government on the problems and needs of legitimate Lowland distillers in Scotland and the all-important Act of 1823 embodied several of his suggestions. His sons carried on distilling at Lochrin and Sunbury until 1849, when these distilleries closed down. His brother John's distillery at Bonnington prospered, and after John's death in 1819 it was continued by *his* sons William, George and Thomas, operating as William Haig and Company. Thomas Haig eventually settled in England and helped to build Hammersmith distillery.

Meanwhile the distillery established at Seggie by James Haig's brother William was flourishing. William became an important figure in St Andrews, of which he was Provost for twelve years. He died in 1847, leaving two sons, John and Robert. Robert took over the management of the distillery at Seggie, but it was John who achieved the most spectacular advance in the fortunes of the Haig family. Already during his father's lifetime he had built a new distillery at Cameron Bridge, Fife (in 1824), and expanded his trade rapidly with the help of 'riders', travelling salesmen who rode all over the country drumming up business and soliciting orders. By 1877 Cameron Bridge distillery was producing 1,250,000 gallons annually. By this time he had long been using the Coffey still. He had erected a Stein still on its first invention (paying a royalty of one penny a gallon to Stein), and soon after Aeneas Coffey's invention of his improved model he had introduced that. Previously he had distilled mostly malt whisky ('malt aqua' as it was called in the trade), but now he produced the cheaper and more plentiful grain whisky.

John Haig of Cameron Bridge inherited his father's

position as spokesman for the Lowland whisky trade before the Government, and several times discussed the question of duties on spirits with Gladstone. He was also much concerned with the whole pattern of distilling in the Lowlands, and it was because of this concern that the Cameron Bridge distillery, as we have seen, was one of the six constituent firms of the Distillers Company Limited when it was founded on 24 April 1877. DCL thus took over the proprietorship of the Cameron Bridge distillery, John Haig and his eldest son Hugh becoming Directors of the new company and a younger son William becoming Secretary. But the blending business of John Haig and Company remained independent, moving from Cameron Bridge to Markinch, only a few miles away, and, with John and his sons Hugh, William and Alexander, operating as John Haig Sons and Co.

The Haigs were thus active both in distilling at Cameron Bridge and in blending at Markinch. John Haig died in 1878 and his son William prematurely in 1884. But the firm continued to prosper. In 1882 it amalgamated with David Smith and Company of Leith in order to obtain the use of their bonded warehouse which they used until 1892 when they established their own bonded warehouse at Markinch. In 1894 John Haig and Company was floated as a limited company, registered in Edinburgh, with John Haig's eldest son Hugh as first Chairman. Hugh died in 1902 and was succeeded as Chairman by his son John.

In 1888 Hugh's brother John Alicius Haig established the separate firm of Haig and Haig Ltd., which specialized in exports to the United States between that date and the advent of prohibition in America in 1920. Haig and Haig remained inactive during the period of prohibition in America, but revived on its repeal in 1933 and resumed its American exports, so that even now, Haig whisky in America until recently had 'Haig and Haig' and not, as in Britain, 'John Haig and Co. Ltd.' on the label of the bottle, though Haig and Haig has been a wholly owned subsidiary of John Haig and Co. since 1925, six years after John Haig and Co. were acquired by DCL. In 1903 John Haig and

Co. acquired the Glen Cawdor distillery to make sure of its own supply of Highland malt whisky for blending. In 1906 the firm were appointed purveyors to the House of Lords. Together with all the other whisky firms they suffered under the restrictions and high taxation of the First World War, under the high taxation of the period between the wars, under the severe restrictions and still higher taxation during the Second World War and its aftermath, and under the even higher taxation of more recent years : these are matters for a later chapter. But in spite of all setbacks the firm has continued to prosper. Like the other great whisky firms that established themselves as blenders and merchandisers of blended Scotch whisky in the latter part of the nineteenth century, Haigs were active in advertising. In the early part of the present century their slogan was 'D'ye ken John Haig?' but this gave way in the late 1920s to the familiar 'Don't be vague – ask for Haig'. At one time Haigs had a yacht which sailed up and down the south coast of England in the holiday season displaying the Haig slogan on its sails. Before the First World War Haigs advertised in Berlin with a trap pulled by two Shetland ponies driven by a Highlander in full panoply.

Facilities at Markinch were much expanded during the present century, with the provision of automatic filling and labelling machinery, additional bottling vats, a new case factory equipped with the latest plant, and other new developments. A fire at one of the stores in December 1928 destroyed old and valuable stocks, but it at least had the advantage of leading to the erection of more modern premises. By 1938, after recovery from the slump of the early 1930s, a tremendous expansion had been carried out, under the energetic managing directorship of Mr William Reid. The new 'coronation Bond' building completed in 1938 provided storage accommodation for over 1,500,000 gallons of whisky and bottling facilities for over 1,750,000 cases annually. It was in the late 1930s, too, that Mr Thomas Wilkinson, then Chairman of the Company, developed exports throughout the world with a vast network of Haig distributors. On the home market, it is the largest selling brand.

The export trade was carried on, under enormous difficulties, during the Second World War. It was a consignment of 2000 cases of Haig and Haig whisky on the SS *Politician* that went down when the ship was wrecked off the Isle of Eriskay in the Outer Hebrides on the way to America. This was the basis of Compton Mackenzie's novel *Whisky Galore* which was made into the brilliant comic film of that title (called *Tight Little Island* in America). In the story and the film the ship was called *The Cabinet Minister*; the actual filming was done on the island of Barra.

At the time of writing, Haig's whisky has been for some years the best-selling Scotch whisky in Britain. (Bell's is the top seller in Scotland.) 'Johnnie Walker' is the over-all leading seller throughout the world.[19]

Haig is the oldest of the 'Big Five', in one sense the most romantic, because of its long history, in another the least romantic because the Haig story is not that of one picturesque character of enormous energy and even flamboyance creating single-handed a great new business. The great self-made men of the Scotch whisky industry are fascinating figures. Let us now take a look at them.

John Dewar was born in 1806 on a small Perthshire farm. When he was twenty-two he went to Perth at the invitation of a relative, James Macdonald, a wine-merchant in that city, to look after the cellars. Dewar was happy in Perth and prospered there. In 1837 he was made a partner in the firm, which was now renamed Macdonald and Dewar. In 1846 he decided to set up on his own, and opened a wine and spirit business in a little single-fronted shop at 111 High Street. There he flourished, soon blending his own whisky and putting it up in bottles, a hitherto unknown refinement. At first he sold principally in Perth and its environs, but gradually he extended his activities. In 1860 he employed a traveller to go farther afield for orders. In 1879 he took his son John Alexander Dewar into partnership. He died in 1880, having established a very comfortable business, soundly based if limited in size and not yet looking beyond Scotland.

It was the next generation that really made whisky history. John Alexander Dewar and his younger brother Thomas Robert had both been carefully trained in the whisky business and had been apprenticed in Leith, by then the centre of the Scotch whisky trade. The two brothers (the elder was only twenty-four when his father died) decided to go for the English market. Tommy Dewar was sent to London by his elder brother, when he was only twenty-one, to get English orders. He knew nobody there: he had in fact two introductions but found on arrival that one of the two people he was to meet was dead and the other was bankrupt. But Tommy triumphed by wit and resourcefulness. In 1886 he startled the Brewers' Show at the Agricultural Hall by drowning out all other sound with the bagpipes and refusing to stop playing when requested. This brought him the initial publicity he wanted. Within a few years he had obtained orders for his bottled blended whisky from a great variety of hotels and restaurants in London. In 1894 Dewars opened a branch in Bristol. The year before Queen Victoria had granted them a Royal Warrant. And by now the firm was acquiring distilleries of its own; the brothers leased from the Duke of Atholl the distillery of Tullymet near Balinluig on upper Tayside, and in 1896 they built their own distillery a few miles away at Aberfeldy, near the croft where the original John Dewar was born in 1806. This distillery still contributes its malt whisky to Dewar's 'White Label'.

It had all been a tremendous gamble, financed by bank overdrafts. But it paid off. In 1894 the firm became a limited liability company with a capital of £100,000, raised to £600,000 in 1897. Tommy Dewar travelled the world setting up agents for the importing of Dewar's whisky. By 1901 Dewars had passed the million-gallon-a-year mark. It was a partnership between these two very different brothers that had achieved this remarkable success. John stayed in Perth and looked after the production end; he was the administrator, while the livelier Tommy was the salesman. It was Tommy who pioneered the flamboyant and enormously successful Dewar advertising. Before 1908, when Dewar House was built in the Haymarket, Dewar's London offices were at Dewar's Wharf on the South Bank of the Thames near Waterloo Bridge, and included the old Shot Tower. On the tower Dewars displayed a huge electric sign showing a bearded Highlander periodically raising to his lips a glass of Dewar's 'White Label' while each time he raised his glass his kilt and beard appeared to sway in the wind. The name DEWAR in enormous letters above the Highlander's tam o' shanter dominated the landscape. A once well-known Dewar advertising slogan was 'The Whisky of his Forefathers', with appropriate picture, another was the series starting with the phrase 'The spirit of . . .'.

Tommy Dewar received a knighthood in 1901 and John a baronetcy in 1907. In 1917 John was raised to the peerage as Baron Forteviot of Dupplin – the first of the 'whisky barons'. Tommy got *his* peerage in 1919, becoming Baron Dewar of Homestall, Sussex. It was not for their services to whisky that they were thus honoured – at least not ostensibly. Each had served his city with distinction. John served as Lord Provost of Perth and Tommy as Sheriff of London. John also served two terms in Parliament as Liberal member for Inverness, while Tommy served as Conservative member for St George's in the East. Tommy was the livelier character. While Lord Forteviot loved his native Perthshire and his estate of Dupplin there, where he died in 1929, Lord Dewar set up as an English country gentleman at Homestall, Sussex. True to the traditions of the English landed gentry, he became a patron of sport and a race-horse owner. Horse-racing, indeed, became his chief hobby, and he bred some famous horses, with one of which, 'Cameronian', his heir and nephew John Arthur Dewar won the Derby in 1931, shortly after his uncle's death in 1930.

After Dewar House was built in 1908 it rapidly became, thanks to Tommy Dewar, a social centre for more than those interested in the whisky trade.[20] Tommy was a wit and a character. He never married, as one of his sayings, 'Do right and fear no man; don't write and fear no woman', suggests. Another of his well-known remarks was: 'The motor car has done away with horses, but not with the ass.'

The work of the brothers was carried on by another Dewar, who was in fact no relation – Peter Menzies Dewar, Chairman of the Company from 1930 to 1946. He was a man of immense energy and ability, who had joined the firm as a boy and was wholly dedicated to it. He did a great deal to expand Dewar's exports and also saw the firm through the difficult days of the Second World War, when their exports to America were of great economic value to the country. In 1946 Peter Dewar was succeeded as Chairman by John Arthur Dewar who was in turn succeeded in 1954 by Henry Evelyn Alexander Dewar, third Lord Forteviot and grandson of the founder. Though Dewars joined DCL in 1925 the firm remained under the administration of the family who founded it.

When in August 1966 John Dewar and Sons were awarded the Queen's Award to Industry, the Earl of Mansfield, who made the presentation on behalf of the Queen, pointed out in his speech that the award was instituted 'in order to encourage and suitably recognize those firms and businesses who are contributing materially to the export trade of this country'. Dewars have indeed a remarkable export record: 90 per cent of all output of whisky is exported. They boast that they export to every market in the world except Albania, Saudi Arabia and the People's Republic of China. They have a promising trade with Soviet Russia. They have agents throughout the world, and even where the sale of alcoholic liquor is conducted by Government monopolies – as in Turkey, Canada, Norway, Sweden, Iceland and Finland – they have agents to supervise their interests and to promote sales. In Britain there are sales offices in London, Liverpool, Leeds, Birmingham and Glasgow to act as intermediaries with merchants and as shipping offices.

Dewar takes second place to John Walker in world-wide whisky sales. But sales of other of the 'Big Five' follow closely behind, with 'Vat 69' making a 'Big Six'.

Dewar's head office is now at Inveralmond, near Perth,

where they have built Scotland's largest plant for blending and bottling whisky. This was opened in June 1962, replacing the former headquarters of the firm at Glasgow Road, Perth. The plant at Inveralmond occupies 24 acres, with 26 acres reserved for expansion. It is an enormous place. Approximately 650 people are employed there. The bottle store holds 2,500,000 bottles and the bottling vats hold up to 110,000 gallons. The plant can fill 200,000 bottles a day of 45 different sizes. Only blending and bottling go on at Inveralmond: it is not a distillery. But to it come for blending whiskies from a great variety of distilleries throughout Scotland, including, of course, Dewar's own distillery at Aberfeldy. Two blends a day are mixed in the blending vats into which compressed air is blown to 'rouse' the mixture. The blend stands for twenty-four hours in the blending vat before being put into plain oak casks to 'marry' over a minimum period of six months.

One more name must be mentioned before I conclude the Dewar story, that of John Alexander Cameron, the man who devised the Dewar's 'White Label' blend. There are various legends about the origin of blending, one of which states that the original John Dewar discovered the art by accident by mixing the remains of empty kegs. This is an invention. It was the firm of Andrew Usher and Co. of Edinburgh who began blending whiskies commercially about 1853 by 'vatting' different Glenlivet whiskies. W. P. Lowrie and Co. of Glasgow were also early in the field with blended whisky. But blending was in the air in the middle of the nineteenth century and increasing later; the French had been mixing old and new brandies for some time. There is a lot of nonsense talked about blending, and blended Scotch whisky may be anything from 80 per cent cheap patent-still whisky to a carefully balanced blend of many different malt whiskies with some 50 per cent patent-still whisky. I shall not anticipate here the discussion of blends and blending that belongs to a later chapter. But I do not want to leave the House of Dewar without recording the name of their distinguished blending expert, John Cameron, one of the pioneers of blending and one of its most remarkable practitioners.

The next great nineteenth-century whisky family to bring on to the stage is the Walkers. Most people are familiar with the advertising slogan of 'Johnnie Walker' whisky – 'Born 1820, still going strong'; and it was in fact in 1820 that John Walker set up as a grocer and wine and spirit merchant in Kilmarnock, Ayrshire. But the whisky associated with his name was not born until some thirty years later. John's business was that of a modest retailer, and it was not until his son Alexander joined him in 1856 that it began to expand and to move from retail to wholesale. In that year Walker, who had survived a disastrous flood in 1852 in which he had lost all his stock, had only one cellar, less than sixty feet long, as his warehouse; within ten years his output was 100,000 gallons of blended whisky and the firm's premises had to be greatly enlarged. This was largely Alexander's doing. He sold his whisky to ships sailing out of Glasgow, and he took advantage of Kilmarnock's reputation as a centre for Brussels, Turkey and Scottish carpets and for tweeds, blankets and shawls to familiarize the English buyers who came there with his Scotch whisky; then he followed them to England and in 1880 opened an office in London. The change from brandy to whisky that I discussed in the previous chapter was now strongly under way, and Alexander Walker arrived in London at a good time. In 1886 Alexander brought his two sons, George and John, into the firm, which now became John Walker and Sons Limited. But it was Alexander's third son Alec who became head of the firm on his father's death in 1889.

Though Alexander Walker was the real founder of the firm as blenders and exporters of Scotch whisky, it was not until long after his death, in 1908, that the brand name 'Johnnie Walker' began to be used in the now well-known slogan. It was invented to accompany a poster by Tom Browne, the painter and black-and-white artist (who also created the American comic characters Weary Willie and Tired Tim). In its earlier history the whisky had been called simply Walker's Kilmarnock Whisky. But Tom

Browne's poster and the accompanying slogan, one of the most successful advertising devices ever known, soon made the name of 'Johnnie Walker' universally known : it is still the best-selling whisky in the world.

If Alexander Walker was the great character who put the Walker firm on the map, it was a local youngster called James Stevenson, who joined the firm in 1890, who played the main part in the later strengthening and expansion. Stevenson was an administrative genius who later was to do important work for munitions production in the First World War and was Surveyor-General of Supply at the War Office from 1919 to 1921; he was also chairman of the board that arranged the great British Empire Exhibition at Wembley in 1924 and 1925. But it was in the years between his joining the firm and the outbreak of the First World War that his greatest services to Walkers were rendered. Working with George and Alec Walker, he succeeded in making the firm the largest blenders and bottlers of Scotch whisky in the world. In 1893 they acquired the malt distillery of Cardow at Knockando near Craigellachie on Speyside : this distillery had been begun by John Cumming in 1824 in the same circumstances which led George Smith to go legitimate at Glenlivet in the same year, and a long history of illegal distilling lay behind it. (Cardhu, a pleasing if not world-shattering Highland malt whisky, has fairly recently become available again as a single whisky.) In 1897 the firm opened a branch in Birmingham, which Stevenson took charge of, and in 1907 they moved their London office to Dunster House, Park Lane.

Stevenson's services to the Government in the First World War won him a baronetcy in 1917 and a peerage (as Baron Stevenson) in 1924. Alec Walker never achieved the peerage and had to make do with a knighthood. He was not the greatest of the whisky magnates, for the pioneering work had been done by his father and the expansion in his own time was largely engineered by Stevenson. But he was an interesting character, with an enormous knowledge of whisky. His training had been both legal, with a firm of

Ayrshire solicitors, and in the whisky trade, for as a young man he had been sent to work with Robertson and Baxter, Glasgow distillers and blenders. Alec's elder brother George became managing director in 1890; in 1912 George, Alec and Stevenson became joint managing directors. By this time their enormous and rapid expansion had raised the bogy of over-production. A few years earlier John Walker and Sons had entered into negotiation with two other members of the 'Big Five', Dewars and Buchanans, with a view to amalgamation in the face of rising competition from DCL and the threat of over-production, but the negotiations did not prove successful. (It was not until 1925 that Walker's, together with Buchanan's and Dewar's, merged with DCL.) The problems brought about by the outbreak of the First World War soon removed the threat of over-production. The firm has survived wars and taxation. Sir Alec Walker survived until 1950, devoting his last years to golf in the Ayrshire town of Troon to which he had retired. Lord Stevenson died in 1926 at the relatively early age of fifty-three.

Johnnie Walker's enormous export business has necessitated a redevelopment of their mode of operation. Their Hill Street premises at Kilmarnock were expanded in the 1950s to develop to the full all the land the company had available, and a new blending plant has recently been built on a 32-acre site near by at Barleith. Blending operations on the one hand and bottling and transportation on the other are now separated, the latter carried out at Hill Street (where as recently as 1955 a new integrated blending, bottling, warehousing and cooperage complex came into operation) and the former at Barleith. The fact that between the mid-1950s and the early 1960s the integrated functions of the new Hill Street building became too much for the space available and necessitated a great new blending plant, is evidence of the rapid strides made in the production and world-wide distribution of Johnnie Walker whisky. The two great bottling halls at Hill Street (like the Dewar bottling hall at Inveralmond) have lines which work automatically, and bottles of many different sizes are mechanically filled, corked, labelled (with different labels for different markets) and, for export to the USA, provided with the strip stamp across the top demanded by the US Customs (these Customs stamps have to be paid for in advance). The warehouse at Barleith can store 15,000 barrels of whisky. At Barleith, too, are the largest blending vats of their kind in the world – three 40,000-gallon stainless-steel-lined vats. In November 1974 DCL announced that the extra capacity required by Johnnie Walker because of its expanding sales would be met by the building of a new blending and bottling complex in Glasgow at an estimated cost for the buildings alone of £8 million, with several more millions for machinery and equipment. The plant will be on a 44-acre site at King George V Dock where there is direct access to the motorways serving central Scotland and the docks. As with Dewar's and others of the world-famous blended Scotch whiskies, the bulk of Johnnie Walker whisky is exported – over 85 per cent of the annual production.

It is always worth looking at the *Dictionary of National Biography* to see what a man's life looks like when it is distilled into a few paragraphs. For this purpose the *Concise DNB* is better still. Stevenson made the *DNB*; none of the Haigs, Dewars or Walkers did. Our next whisky magnate, however, was more successful. His brief entry in the *Concise DNB*, 1901–50 is an ironic commentary on his life and character : 'BUCHANAN, JAMES, BARON WOOLAVINGTON (1849–1935), philanthropist and race-horse owner; made a fortune as a distiller of whisky; won St Leger (1916) with Hurry On, Derby (1922) with Captain Cuttle, and both races and Eclipse Stakes (1926) with Coronach; benefactor of British Museum, Edinburgh University, Middlesex Hospital, etc.; baronet, 1920; baron, 1922; GCVO, 1931.' Philanthropist and race-horse owner! The fourteen-year-old youngster working as an office boy in the Glasgow shipping firm of William Sloan & Co. for a salary of £10 a year (rising to £15 the second year and to £20 in the third year of his initial three-year contract) would hardly have recognized *that* description. For Buchanan really was a self-made man. Born in Canada in 1849 of Scottish emigrant parents, he had been brought back to Scotland as an infant and then lived for some time with his parents in Northern Ireland. He joined the Glasgow shipping firm in 1863. After his first three years there he became a Custom House and clearing clerk, working very long hours for no increase in pay, though the normal pay for such a clerk was £60 to £70 a year. So he left, and at the age of nineteen joined his brother in his grain business in Glasgow. Here he remained for nearly ten years, gaining experience of grain that was to lead him to an interest in distilling.

In 1879 Buchanan got himself a job as London agent for the Leith whisky-merchants and blenders, Charles Mackinlay & Co. Five years later, sniffing a whisky boom in the air, he founded his own firm of James Buchanan & Co. at 61 Basinghall Street, London. He was now thirty-five years old, venturesome, ambitious, confident – and virtually without capital. He was shrewd, too, and knew of the commercial advantages involved in marketing in England a blend of malt whiskies and patent-still grain whiskies. W. P. Lowrie, chairman of W. P. Lowrie & Co., a Glasgow whisky firm which had early gone into blending, supplied him with stocks of whisky. Lowrie owned the Convalmore distillery in Dufftown (still going strong), a Highland malt distillery which Buchanan himself later bought; Lowrie also owned Glentauchers distillery in Mulben, Banffshire. (On Mr Lowrie's retirement in 1906 Buchanan took over his firm, though it still retains the Lowrie name.) 'What I made up my mind to do,' Buchanan wrote years later as Lord Woolavington, 'was to find a blend sufficiently light and old to please the palate of the user. This I fortunately was able to do, and I made rapid headway. I need hardly say that I was on the quest for business night and day, getting instructions and getting to know people wherever I could.' In his old age Lord Woolavington wondered how he had done it: 'When I think sometimes I marvel at the supreme self-confidence that upheld me – a young man without capital and practically no knowledge of the business I was embarking in; a stranger in the City of London. The extraordinary thing is that the possibility of failure never once occurred to me. I had it always before me in my mind that sooner or later I was bound to make a success.'

Buchanan first set about selling his product with whisky blended from stocks obtained from Lowrie. He put it in a black bottle with a white label and went about selling it with enormous panache. A gay, irrepressible, resourceful character, Buchanan reminds one a bit of Tommy Dewar, but he had even more charm and spirit than his brilliant rival from Perth. By every kind of stratagem, ranging from deliberately cultivating the acquaintance of hotel and restaurant owners to squiring the daughters of a rich whisky buyer, he got his orders. He got the contract for the supply of whisky to the London music halls and was the first whisky supplier to get a contract to supply whisky to the House of Commons Bar. He called his whisky 'Buchanan's Blend'[21] at first, then put 'House of Commons' in larger letters on the label. In March 1904 the registered design of the label was altered to 'Buchanan's Special' and later in the same year he registered the name 'Black and White' which, because of the black bottle and the white label, had already for some time been the unofficial name by which customers had asked for it. In 1898 Buchanan bought the famous Black Swan distillery in Holborn, which he rebuilt on borrowed money. Everything he touched prospered. His whisky moved about London in splendid drays drawn by magnificent horses with the drivers in spectacular olde Englishe uniforms. They were one of the sights of London until they were replaced by motor vans in 1936.

In the fifteen years before the First World War broke out Buchanan's business expanded rapidly. He opened branches in England and on the Continent; he secured royal patronage from both Edward VII and George V. He exported to Europe, North and South America and New Zealand. The firm became a limited liability company in 1903, but characteristically Buchanan kept the shares in his own hands: until 1915 the firm remained a one-man show. Like the other big whisky firms, he had his difficulties during the war, and in 1915 amalgamated with Dewars as a means of solving some of these. Both Dewars and Buchanans

joined DCL in 1925. Buchanans moved their head office to
Devonshire House, Piccadilly, in 1953.

In the decade before the outbreak of the First World
War Buchanan brought himself to public notice by his
strong advocacy of military preparedness. He founded the
Buchanan Rifle Club in 1905 and encouraged his employees
to train. He was raised to the peerage as Baron Woolavington of Lavington in 1922. By that time he had long been
widely known as a sportsman. Like Tommy Dewar, he
became an English country gentleman with an estate in
Sussex and took up race-horse breeding with the success
referred to in the *DNB* entry I began by quoting. As the
DNB says, Buchanan made a fortune out of whisky. He was
a great *entrepreneur* rather than a great whisky expert. In
a way he was almost a caricature of the self-made capitalist
whose heyday was more in late nineteenth-century America
than in Britain. But everyone who knew him agreed that
he was a most attractive character. If it could not be said of
him, as Dr Johnson said of Garrick, that his death 'eclipsed
the gaiety of nations', at least it could be argued that his life
contributed to the gaiety of nations, not only by his production of vast quantities of whisky but by his personality and
the colour and vivacity with which he conducted his business. He was almost eighty-six when he died in 1935, active
until the end, in spite of having broken a thigh eleven years
before. By that time his days of lively pioneering in whisky
salesmanship were long behind him, and he was mourned
as a great sportsman and philanthropist.

The last of the 'Big Five' whisky firms is 'White Horse'
which, contrary to what some of the advertisements suggest,
has no historical connection at all with the White Horse Inn
in the Canongate, Edinburgh, where Boswell is erroneously
supposed to have met Dr Johnson at the beginning of the
latter's Highland jaunt. The firm was founded in Glasgow
by James Logan Mackie in 1883. Mackie had had experience as a distiller in Islay and he and his partner, Captain
Graham, decided to make a blend of the great Islay malt
whisky Lagavulin, an Eastern malt whisky from Craigellachie distillery, and patent-still grain whisky. The charac-

teristic peatiness of the Lagavulin gave the blend a highly distinctive flavour. (Lagavulin is still used in 'White Horse', and its flavour is still discernible, but many other whiskies are also now used in the blending and the blend is not identical with what it once was.) James Logan Mackie and Co., as the firm was called, decided to call their blend 'White Horse', and it was James's nephew, Peter Mackie, who succeeded his uncle on the latter's retirement in 1890, who effectively exploited the various historical and symbolic associations of the name. James was the founder, Peter the *entrepreneur* who built up the firm into one of the great whisky firms of the world : the story is by now a familiar one. Peter had been trained as a distiller at Lagavulin distillery, which his uncle took over in 1888 (Peter bought Craigellachie distillery in 1915). In 1891 Mackie and Co. became a limited liability company and the name 'White Horse' was officially registered.

The story now becomes one of continuous expansion. Into the by now highly competitive world of blended Scotch whisky Peter Mackie brought a blend of highly distinctive flavour and pushed it with all the devices of advertising that were so characteristic of the whisky trade. He was created a baronet in 1920, and died in 1924, the year when the firm of Mackie and Co. was dissolved to be replaced by White Horse Distillers Ltd. It was shortly after the reconstruction of the company under this new title that White Horse introduced screw caps for their bottles instead of corks – a revolution in whisky bottling which sharply accelerated their sales.

Bruce Lockhart has described Peter Mackie as 'one-third genius, one-third megalomaniac and one-third eccentric'. He boasted of his Highland blood and loved to parade in full Highland dress. He was an ardent Tory politician and a great supporter of imperial preference. He loved to shoot over the moors and wrote an authoritative book on the subject. He was always full of schemes, and diversified his activities in some rather odd ways, including milling a special health-giving flour and weaving tweed. He was always very much the boss and ruled his employees with benevolent despotism. Like most of the other Scotch whisky magnates, he resisted amalgamation with DCL as long as he could and in fact kept White Horse Distillers out of DCL during his lifetime. It was only after his death, in 1927, that DCL acquired control of White Horse and William Ross's dream of seeing all the 'Big Five' inside his company was finally realized.

These, then, were the 'Big Five' of blended Scotch whisky whose activities helped to revolutionize the Scotch whisky industry in the latter part of the nineteenth and the first part of the twentieth century. There were, of course, many other firms, as there still are, playing an important part in the Scotch whisky trade. Some of these will be mentioned when I discuss the quality of some individual whiskies. One, however, really deserves a place here beside the 'Big Five' for its importance in the history of blended Scotch whisky. This is the firm of William Sanderson Ltd., founded by William Sanderson of Leith in May 1863. It was as a wine and cordial manufacturer that Sanderson started: under Gladstone's Act of 1860 he could make and sell wholesale (but not retail) any fermented liquor made from fruit and sugar for a licence fee of five guineas and he could also do his own rectifying for an additional licence fee of ten guineas. He experimented with different cordials and mixtures. The first entry in his record book reads as follows:

MIXTURE WHISKY
10 gallons Glenlivet, 10 gallons Pitlochry
5 gallons Reduced mixed Aqua [i.e. whisky]
8 gallons Grain
4 gallons water, $\frac{1}{2}$ gallon aqua Shrub
8 gallons Grain Aqua

The next year, in 1864, Sanderson noted in his record book the improvement produced by maturing whisky in sherry casks, and heavily underlined the observations. He went on experimenting with a variety of mixtures – Ginger Cordial, Rhubarb Wine, Raspberry Cordial, and many others. And he tried various kinds of 'Aqua Shrub', a compounded drink made of fruit juice, sugar and whisky. He also made a 'Whisky Bitters', a drink which, as I noted in chapter 1, remained popular well into the present century. He travelled Scotland seeking buyers for his products. He began to export to the Continent. He prospered and bought himself a fine new house in Ferry Road which he called Talbot House because the Talbot Hound had been the badge of his Border ancestors. (The Talbot Hound is still impressed on the seal of every bottle of 'Vat 69'.)

William Sanderson was a friend of John Begg, who owned Royal Lochnagar distillery above Balmoral Castle on Deeside. Queen Victoria and Prince Albert had visited the distillery and sampled its product in 1848. Lochnagar was one of the main malt whiskies used by Sanderson in his mixtures. He became more and more interested in mixing (or, as we would now say, blending) whiskies and noted his experiments in a cash book headed 'Adventures in Aqua'. In 1876 he took out a licence as a spirit dealer. In 1880 he was joined in the business by his son William Mark Sanderson. It was William Mark who, taking advantage of the fact that Leith had long been noted for its manufacture of glass bottles, persuaded his father to sell his blends in bottles rather than in barrels to ensure that they were not tampered with by the retailer or publican. By this time both Sandersons were sure that the future of the firm depended on their production of blended Scotch whisky : the problem now was to fix on a suitable blend. William Sanderson was a born experimenter, and might have gone on trying out new blends for ever if (one suspects – but this is guesswork) his son had not insisted that they choose a first-rate blend and make that their principal merchandise. The story goes that in July 1882 Sanderson made up nearly a hundred different blends of malt and grain whiskies, putting each into a numbered small cask or vat. Then he invited a number of expert blenders and friends to taste them and select the best. Their choice – and it was Sanderson's own as well – was unanimously the blended whisky in the vat numbered 69. And so 'Vat 69' was born.

The year 1877 had seen the birth of DCL. Worried by

the competition and anxious to secure their supplies of grain whisky, William Sanderson and a number of other whisky merchants and blenders decided to form a company that would set up their own patent-still distillery. The company was formed in October 1885, with Sanderson as Managing Director, Andrew Usher as Chairman, and, as directors, John M. Crabbie, George Robertson, John Somerville, James McLennan and Alex. Murdoch. The company called itself the North British Distillery Company Ltd. and their distillery opened at Gorgie, Edinburgh, in 1887.[22] In 1886 Sanderson became co-owner of the Glengarioch malt distillery, Old Meldrum, Aberdeenshire. He could thus count on the North British grain whisky, Glengarioch malt whisky, and John Begg's Lochnagar malt whisky.

For some time Sanderson kept a variety of blends on the market instead of concentrating all his efforts on 'Vat 69'. He had a blend for morning drinking called 'A.M.' and one for postmeridian drinking called 'P.M.'. He had his 'S.V.G.' or 'Specially Vatted Glengarioch', his 'I.M.' containing a high proportion of Islay whisky, his 'Special', 'Extra Special' and others. He also tried out a 'Vat 88' which had a degree of success for some time. And he produced a Whisky Bitters described on the label as 'A Drink, not a Flavouring Extract, The King of Tonic Drinks, A Pick-me-up and Appetiser. May be taken as a liqueur, or with plain or aerated water. Made with very fine Scotch Whisky of great age.' But as the firm grew, 'Vat 69' came more and more to the fore. By 1903, when William Sanderson's youngest son Arthur Watson Sanderson joined the firm (now 'William Sanderson and Son, Distillers and Scotch Whisky Merchants'), the most exotic of the firm's activities had been allowed to dwindle, and whisky, particularly 'Vat 69', was its main output.

William Sanderson died in 1908 and was succeeded by his son William Mark. The concentration was now on exports, already considerable to Australia, South Africa and Canada and now extended to Denmark, Sweden, Germany, Belgium and France. The first consignment to America was shipped in March 1908. William Mark introduced the advertising slogan 'Quality Tells!' and 'Vat 69' continued to boom. In 1917 Sandersons took over the eighty-year-old firm of whisky-merchants Carstairs and Robertson and in 1920 the old Leith firm of wine and spirit merchants D. and G. McLaren. After the First World War, with all its problems, Sandersons resisted amalgamation with DCL and in fact held out until 1937, when amalgamation took place.

The firm incorporated as a limited liability company in 1925 with William Mark Sanderson as Chairman. He died in 1929 and was succeeded as Chairman by his son Kenneth. In 1933 Sandersons amalgamated with Booth's Distilleries Ltd., a firm which already owned the Stromness distillery in Orkney, the Royal Brackla distillery in Nairn, and Millburn distillery near Inverness, all fine malt-whisky distilleries. Kenneth Sanderson (whose great hobby was motor racing) devoted himself to extending exports and travelled widely for this purpose. Finally, as I have mentioned, the growing rationalization of the whole Scotch whisky trade brought Booths and Sandersons into DCL in 1937. In 1962 the firm moved their London office to a new building in Stanhope Gate, by Park Lane.

The Sanderson story is an interesting family saga which really goes back to old Captain Mark Sanderson, Leith sea captain who died in 1832. The restless curiosity of William Sanderson and more single-minded business acumen of his son William Mark are both important parts of the story. None of the Sandersons has the flamboyance and extrovert charm of Tommy Dewar or James Buchanan. But we have the feeling that their interest centred genuinely on whisky (or on 'whisky mixtures') and that they were whisky men rather than financial wizards. This is not to say that the 'Big Five' were not whisky men too, but some of them were *entrepreneurs* who happened to have chosen whisky as their product and who could have done just as well with anything else. One does not get that feeling about the Sandersons.

Talking some years ago to a Director of one of the 'Big Five', I was interested to hear him say that the great whisky barons of the late nineteenth century not only represented a kind of individual enterprise impossible today but also pursued a way of life which if attempted now might well land the pursuer in gaol. He was not suggesting for a moment that the founding fathers of the whisky trade were crooks, but he was emphasizing that the conditions under which business firms now operate are much more hedged round with legal restrictions than they used to be. The kind of financial risks which those old boys took might easily result in involvement with the law today. He mentioned as an example the name of a would-be builder of an industrial empire who was at the time of our conversation awaiting trial on complicated charges involving financial manipulation of a kind that earlier, if it eventually resulted in success, would have escaped any legal enquiry. The other important thing to remember about the 'Big Five' is that they pioneered a lively and imaginative advertising which has had a permanent influence on trade practices. As a later chapter will show, I am highly critical of some aspects of modern whisky advertising; but I cannot help admiring the gaiety, the debonair quality, the splendid dash and vigour of much of that pioneering advertising. Whisky, after all, is not like the majority of commercial products. Its primary function is to increase pleasure, and an awareness of this in the whisky trade must be what accounts for that special air of friendliness and relaxation that I have found among whisky men.

5

War and Taxes

The Scotch whisky boom of the 1890s came to an end with
the Pattison failure of 1898. After that the number of working distilleries in Scotland began to decline – from 161 in
1898 to 149 in 1902 and 122 in 1910. As we have seen, the
Distillers Company Ltd. (DCL), by its policy of amalgamation and controlled production, fought continuously to
prevent Scotch whisky from being caught up in a boom-and-
recession cycle. This policy was especially fostered by
Graham Menzies, who became Chairman of DCL in 1897,
and William Ross, who held the combined office of General
Manager and Secretary. Ross became Managing Director
in 1900, at the age of thirty-eight, and Chairman in 1925,
continuing in the latter position until his retirement in 1935,
in spite of a serious accident in 1917 which fractured one
leg and seriously damaged the other, and the onset of total
blindness in 1931 as a result of an accident on shipboard
two years before. It was Ross who negotiated the formation
in 1899 of the United Yeast Company Ltd. as a DCL
subsidiary and so both safeguarded Britain's bread supply
and enabled British distillers to survive the cutting off of
yeast imports from the Continent at the beginning of the
First World War. It was Ross who, just before the start of
the First World War, took the lead in forming Scottish
Malt Distillers Ltd., originally a concentration of the
resources of five Lowland malt distillers (of which three still
operate), but since 1930 the organization through which
DCL controls its 41 malt distilleries in Scotland. It was
Ross who fought unremittingly to bring the great blending
firms into DCL and who had his reward in 1925 when
Buchanan-Dewar (these two had merged in 1915) and John
Walker & Sons amalgamated with DCL on the basis of an
exchange of the shares of each of the three companies.
It was Ross, indeed, who could without exaggeration be said

to be the man who enabled the Scotch whisky trade to survive the First World War. The British Government, or at least the Chancellor of the Exchequer, Lloyd George, was seriously considering imposing prohibition on the country after the outbreak of war in order to prevent workers' efficiency from being impaired by alcohol. Ross went to see Lloyd George and explained some of the facts of life to him – the tie-up of the manufacture of yeast (necessary for the baking of bread) with distilling, the industrial and military uses of alcohol. A conference called by the Government in 1915 were told of the dire necessity to conserve grain because of the growing damage to imports done by German submarines. Distilling was, therefore, severely restricted and spirits rationed. In the same year the Immature Spirits (Restriction) Act was passed, prohibiting delivery of whisky for consumption in Britain unless it had matured in a bonded warehouse for a minimum period of three years.

The Immature Spirits (Restriction) Act was intended as a wartime measure, but in fact it has remained law, with unexpected consequences for the future of Scotch whisky. Lloyd George saw it as a means of restricting the consumption of whisky. But James Stevenson, the director of John Walker & Sons who now had a high administrative position in the Ministry of Munitions, persuaded Lloyd George (then Minister of Munitions) to support this legislation (rather than impose prohibition on the country) on the grounds that it was cheap, raw whisky that caused drunkenness among workers, not mature whisky. Stevenson, in fact, seized the opportunity to turn restrictive legislation to the benefit of whisky. The fact is that cheap, new patent-still grain spirit had for some time been a curse in the cities. For hopeless workers in gloomy city slums such whisky, before the war, had provided a quick and destructive way out of misery. The availability of this cheap, raw spirit did not do the reputation of Scotch whisky any good, and Lloyd George's Act, whatever his intentions may have been, has done nothing but good to the Scotch whisky trade. It was not immediately seen in this way, of course. The immediate effect was a great increase in the price of whisky to the consumer. Many independent firms involved in blending and distributing whisky were forced out of business, and their valuable stocks often came into the hands of DCL or their associates. The total cessation of distilling in 1917 further weakened the independent firms and strengthened the case for amalgamation. Further, while the grain distilleries in the DCL group produced industrial alcohol for war purposes, the independent malt distillers did not, and had to close. Thus weakened, these distilleries were in no position to cope with the difficult position of the immediate post-war years, and so a great number of them agreed to amalgamation proposals by DCL. However we look at the picture, it is clear that the First World War and its consequences accelerated the drive towards amalgamation in the Scotch whisky industry and provided new opportunities for DCL. But it was the genius of William Ross that enabled DCL to take advantage of these opportunities. After the great Buchanan-Dewar and John Walker merger with DCL, White Horse Distillers Ltd. came in in 1927. William Sanderson and Son Ltd. ('Vat 69') came into DCL in 1937; A. & A. Crawford (a distinguished Leith blending firm whose 'Three Star' and 'Five Star' whiskies have long been highly esteemed blends) in 1944, and John Crabbie and Company Ltd. (an old-established blending firm, originally grain-whisky distillers and one of the original six in the 1856 trade arrangement of patent-still distillers) in 1963.

Meanwhile, the duty on whisky kept going up. At the beginning of the First World War the price in the United Kingdom of a bottle of one of the proprietary brands of blended Scotch whisky was between 4s and 4s 6d, with the excise duty standing at 14s 9d per proof gallon. In 1918 the duty was raised to 30s per proof gallon, and the retail price of whisky rose from 8s to 9s 6d per bottle. In 1919 the duty rose again to 50s and the retail price to 10s 6d. From 1920 until the outbreak of the Second World War in September 1939 the duty was 72s 6d per proof gallon and the retail price 12s 6d per bottle. In September 1939 the duty went up to £4 2s 6d and from then it has climbed steadily – to £6 17s 6d in 1942; £7 17s 6d in 1943; £9 10s 10d in 1947; £11 11s 11d in 1961; £12 17s 6d in 1964; £14 12s in 1965; £16 1s 3d in 1967; and £17 2s 9d in 1968. In November 1968 it was raised to £18 17s, which made the duty on a standard bottle of blended Scotch whisky £2 4s (or £2.20 in the decimal currency introduced into Britain in 1971).

The introduction of Value Added Tax in April 1973 (initially at 10%) involved a reduction of excise duty to £15.45 per proof gallon, which meant that the duty on a standard bottle was now £1.80 plus 10% of the retail price. In March 1974 the duty per proof gallon was raised to £17.01, making the duty on a bottle £1.98 plus 10% of the retail price. In July 1974 VAT was reduced to 8%. The excise duty is paid only once, when the whisky is withdrawn from bond, whereas VAT is charged as a percentage of the price charged by the distiller or blender to his first customer and again at each subsequent re-sale. (As with all VAT taxation, at each stage the vendor passes on to Customs and Excise the amount of VAT he charges the purchaser, less the amount of VAT he himself has paid to his supplier.)

The combination of excise duty and VAT now included in the price of a bottle of whisky, with each calculated and paid in a different way, makes it difficult for the ordinary retail purchaser in Britain to know how the price he pays is made up. In March 1975 the lowest price for a bottle of blended Scotch whisky was £2.55, and sometimes one saw a special offer of a few pence less even than that. But with excise duty £1.98 a bottle and VAT at 8% of the combined purchase price and duty, even a retail price of £2.55 would not have been profitable. Most whisky in Britain today leaves the producer at about 42p a bottle: add to this the duty of £1.98 and 8% VAT on the resulting retail price of £2.40 and you get a final retail price of £2.59, which means that a retail price of £2.55 was a 'loss leader'. (And this assumes that there is no intermediate price rise between the producer and the retailer: the retailer is indeed often a large chain of grocery shops or wine and spirit merchants, sometimes associated with other firms in a powerful group, which buys direct from the blender.) No wonder that there was a demand in the trade for an increase in the price for the domestic market. Increase in cereal prices, and a huge increase in fuel costs after the Middle East crisis of October 1973, together with industrial action by some distillery workers in 1974 to secure additional pay in the face of rapidly rising inflation, all pointed to a higher price for whisky in Britain. 'The present price,' said Mr David Grant of William Grant and Sons Ltd. ('Standfast' and 'Glenfiddich' and 'Balvenie') in December 1974, 'is suicidal to an industry which employs 23,000 people in Scotland and earned £26m. abroad last year.' It therefore came as no surprise when at the beginning of April 1975 DCL announced a rise of 10 pence on every bottle of their whiskies. And on 16 April 1975 the Chancellor of the Exchequer announced a massive increase in excise duty that put 64 pence on to the price of every bottle of whisky, so that, with VAT at 8%, a bottle of whisky on the domestic market now costs a minimum of £3.30.

The Second World War inevitably brought serious problems to the Scotch whisky trade. The Ministry of Food informed the distillers that the production of whisky would cease at the end of 1939. The six months' stocks of cereal held by DCL for distilling were requisitioned. Three short periods of distilling were allowed up to 1944, when a restricted supply of home-grown cereals were allocated for the manufacture of Scotch whisky for export. Rationing of Scotch whisky for the home market began on 1 March 1940 – each wholesaler was allowed a percentage of what he had bought in the year ending 29 February 1940. In 1940–1 the percentage allowed was 41; it was reduced to 20 in 1948–50. The reason for the severe restriction after the war was over was the desperate need to export. The exports of whisky went on, under most difficult conditions, throughout the war : they were especially high in 1940, reaching £10,470,000. After the 'lend-lease' agreement with America the need to export to pay for needed imports was not quite so desperate and there was a slight decline.

After the end of the Second World War the Ministry of Food continued to allocate cereals for distilling, but the amount gradually increased. There is a famous minute of Mr Churchill's in April 1945 : 'On no account reduce the barley for whisky. This takes years to mature, and is an invaluable export and dollar producer. Having regard to all our other difficulties about exports, it would be most improvident not to preserve this characteristic British element of ascendancy.' The characteristic British element was preserved, and whisky exports flourished while the consumers at home had to make do with the allocation allowed by an agreement between the Ministry of Food, the Board of Trade and the Scotch Whisky Association[23] which, from 1947 to 1953, specified what proportion of the output of Scotch whisky annually should go for export and what should be made available at home. The sort of proportions involved is indicated by the fact that in 1953 11,000,000 proof gallons was set as the export objective (actually exceeded by more than 2,000,000 gallons) and 2,750,000 for the home market. It was not until 1954 that the quota system for domestic consumers was discontinued, but even then stocks had been run down to such an extent that it was 1959 before whisky rationing for the home market (by the whisky trade now, not by the Government) was completely discontinued.

According to DCL statistics issued in July 1974, the sales of the whole of the Scotch Whisky Industry for the years 1964 to 1973 were (in proof gallons) as shown in the table below.

Stocks of whisky have been steadily building up, and by 1974 they reached 1,016,400 proof gallons.

The USA is by far the largest importer of Scotch whisky. In 1973 the USA imported 32,943,000 proof gallons. Japan, which imported 348,000 proof gallons in 1964, expanded its imports rapidly to become the second largest importer of Scotch whisky after America in 1973, with an import of 6,538,000 proof gallons. In 1973 Italy came next with 3,684,000 proof gallons, then France with 3,296,000 and West Germany with 2,918,000. The major proportion of

Year ended 30 Sept.	Production (in proof gallons)
1964	108,091,000
1965	126,455,000
1966	134,471,000
1967	123,971,000
1968	113,606,000
1969	125,999,000
1970	141,935,000
1971	147,518,000
1972	167,638,000
1973	181,541,000

Home and Export Sales (in thousands of proof gallons)
Calendar

Year	Home	%	Export	%	Total	%
1964	9,248	+ 6·7	35,019	+10·2	44,267	+ 9·5
1965	9,035	− 2·3	39,667	+13·3	48,702	+10·0
1966	9,048	+ 0·1	41,597	+ 4·9	50,664	+ 4·0
1967	9,184	+ 1·5	43,146	+ 3·7	52,330	+ 3·3
1968	9,829	+ 7·0	59,155	+37·1	68,984	+31·8
1969	9,233	− 6·1	52,427	−11·4	61,660	−10·6
1970	10,535	+14·1	62,010	+18·3	72,545	+17·7
1971	11,087	+ 5·2	70,328	+13·4	81,415	+12·2
1972	12,583	+13·5	68,752	−2·2	81,335	− 0·1
1973	15,347	+22·0	78,449	+14·1	93,796	+15·3

the Japanese imports was of malt whisky in bulk for blending with Japanese whisky.

A tour of Highland malt distilleries in October 1967 showed many of them working a seven-day week, round the clock. Old distilleries had been modernized, distilleries long out of commission had been put back to work (e.g. Port Ellen distillery, Islay, closed in 1930 and reconstructed in the 1960s; Benriach, Elgin, closed between 1903 and 1965, then re-opened; Caperdonich distillery, Rothes, closed in 1901, re-opened in 1965, and then enlarged and modernized); new distilleries were built (e.g. Tormore at Advie, Morayshire; on the Island of Jura; Loch Lomond distillery, a £1,000,000 complex of distillery, warehousing, bottling plant and cooperage, opened in September 1967, at Alexandria, Dunbartonshire); great new bottling halls and blending warehouses had been built (in addition to those of Dewar and Johnnie Walker, already described, there is Arthur Bell and Sons' vast new one near Broxburn, West Lothian).

The expansion continued into the 1970s. In 1972 DCL opened a new Highland malt distillery, Mannochmore, with an annual capacity of one million proof gallons. It adjoins the company's Glenlossie distillery at Birnie, Morayshire, but draws its water from a different source. DCL also built a new malt whisky distillery at Brora, Sutherland, adjoining Clynelish distillery (it is called simply Brora). Caol Ila distillery on Islay has been rebuilt. Major mechanical maltings have been built, at Ord distillery, Beauly, and Hillside distillery, Montrose, with a slightly smaller one at Port Ellen, Islay, to serve three Islay distilleries (Port Ellen, Caol Ila and Lagavulin) run by Scottish Malt Distillers Ltd., which since 1930 has run all the malt distilleries owned by DCL companies. In 1973 DCL's new subsidiary, The Distillers Company (Bottling Services) Ltd., opened a major blending and bottling complex in Leven, Fife, where the brands of minor companies in the DCL group are mostly blended and bottled. Other developments include a £14m. expansion of its Scotch whisky interests announced at the end of 1974 by Distillers Corporation–Seagrams, to include a new bottling complex on a 50-acre site at Darnley, to the south of Glasgow, and a new distillery, Allt-A-Bhainne, as well as expansion of their existing recently built distillery Braes of Glenlivet. Other new distilleries have been opened at Ledaig (Ledaig Distillery (Tobermory) Ltd., Mull), Auchriosk (International Distillers and Vintners, Rothes) and Pittyvaich (A. Bell & Sons Ltd., Dufftown).

The hundreds of millions of proof gallons of whisky now stocked represent, of course, an enormous investment. Everything must be planned ahead. The whisky that is being distilled now will not come on to the market for some years; but the amount distilled now determines what will be available then. If distillers expand production, as they had been doing in recent years, it means that the big firms who blend and sell the whisky are demanding this : a distillery does not fill casks 'on spec'; for the most part it fills casks sent to it by the blenders, who keep the whisky maturing in the distillery until they want it (occasionally they will sell it to another blender who is short of that particular whisky for his blend : whisky firms are generous in helping each other out in this way). When malt distillers shorten their summer shut-down and work a seven-day week (instead of the traditional Monday to Saturday) they do so in order to fill specific orders. Those orders in turn are based on forecasts (and hopes) by the firms who blend and sell the whisky. To make these forecasts come true, high-powered selling campaigns (especially in America) are necessary and in addition new areas for export have to be found.

Although the bulk of whisky distilled in the great distilleries is now done to order, a small amount is bought by speculators whose aim is to sell it at a profit to a blender in sudden need of it. There are also whisky brokers, important middlemen who hold stocks of whisky and mediate between distillers and blenders so as to provide the latter with what they want when they want it. For blenders cannot always foresee their needs as they would like to. It is still open to private individuals to buy whisky in the cask as an investment, as periodical advertisements in *The Times* make clear. One holds it until it matures and hopes to be able to sell it to a blender at a profit. But it can be dangerous to people not brought up in the whisky trade to get involved in it, and some notable investors in whisky have had their fingers burnt.

Although expansion of distilling and the building of blending and bottling facilities continued into the 1970s, by the beginning of 1975 the picture had begun to change. In December 1974 the Chairman of DCL (which, it must be remembered, is responsible for about six of every ten bottles of Scotch whisky sold throughout the world), after referring to problems caused by unofficial strikes in support of pay claims, other disputes curtailing the transport of materials inwards and of cased goods outwards, and a shortage of bottles and other packaging materials, went on to observe that with the long-term capital market virtually closed, the company had to keep its forward planning within the resources available. 'It will be necessary therefore,' he said, 'to reduce distillation of Scotch whisky in 1975. Hitherto production levels have been designed to cover projected increases in the volume of sales resulting from the continuing expansion in the demand for Scotch whisky together with substantial reserves of stock to meet possible eventualities. A reduction in distillation can therefore be effected whilst maintaining stocks at a level which is entirely adequate to support the forecast increase in demand for our major brands.'

While the increasingly heavy taxation of whisky in the home market has had the effect of holding down domestic consumption, the fact remains that the home market takes more Scotch whisky than any single foreign country except the United States, as the figures given on pages 116–17 show clearly. Still, what has kept the Scotch whisky trade flourishing is its massive exports. Scotland no longer keeps its great spirit to itself. Among the marginal notes written by the actress Ellen Terry in a special interleaved copy of *Macbeth* prepared by Henry Irving for the Irving–Terry production of the play in 1888 there is this comment on Lady Macbeth's line : 'But in them Nature's copy's not eterne' (III. ii. 38). Lady Macbeth is replying to Macbeth's complaint that Banquo and his son Fleance, potential rivals for the throne, are still alive, and is suggesting that they might both be murdered. Or at least that is how most people would construe her observation. But Ellen Terry interpreted the line to mean this : 'Don't trouble so, for they cannot live for ever – that fellow Banquo may die any day – *why not!* and the boy may have whooping cough in such a climate as this – we keep all the whisky to ourselves – I lock up the cupboard every night.' In 1888 Ellen Terry assumed that of course the Macbeths would have had whisky in the palace and that it would have been a good cure for whooping cough. Her reference to whisky reflects the growing awareness of it in the 1880s but also suggests that it was still regarded by many people as primarily medicinal in function (like the 'whisky bitters' still common in the nineteenth century). The medicinal properties of whisky were debated in the House of Commons during the Second World War, and it was agreed that if it did not cure colds it undoubtedly helped the sufferer to endure one in greater comfort. It is certainly good for certain cardiac conditions and helps to prevent coronary thrombosis. But the part of Ellen Terry's comment to which I want to draw attention is her parenthetical 'we keep all the whisky to ourselves'. This was presumably advice given by Lady Macbeth to her husband for sinister power purposes. But it is precisely the fact that the Scots have not kept all the whisky to themselves that has determined its history since Ellen Terry's day.

6

Whisky as a World Drink

The Distillers Company Limited began in 1877 as a combination of six Lowland patent-still distilleries. Although the company built its first malt distillery in the 1890s (at Knockdhu, Banffshire) it was not until the present century that it moved significantly into the fields of blending and of malt-whisky distilling, largely in response to the difficulties faced by the Scotch whisky trade in the First World War. We have seen the important part played by Mr W. H. Ross of DCL in founding Scottish Malt Distillers Limited in 1914. In 1915 DCL and John Walker jointly acquired Coleburn distillery (south of Elgin) and in 1916 Dewar, DCL, W. P. Lowrie (the firm from which James Buchanan originally obtained his stocks of whisky, subsequently bought by Buchanan) and Walker jointly bought the company which operated the malt distilleries of Dailuaine (on Speyside) and Talisker (in Skye). About the same time DCL bought the Glasgow blending firms of John Begg and John Hopkins and the old-established Edinburgh firm of J. & G. Stewart (with which the firm of Andrew Usher, a pioneer of blending, is now incorporated) in order to develop its export trade in blended whisky which it had been conducting on a small scale as an inheritance from Kirkliston distillery, one of the original six in DCL. The opening of the North British grain distillery in 1887 spurred DCL to further efforts in the export field : the company built a blending and bottling warehouse at South Queensferry and marketed 'King George IV' and 'Highland Nectar' through its Export Branch and, later, through the Distillers Agency Ltd. But all this was still on a small scale until the take-overs and mergers that began during the First World War enabled DCL to increase steadily its blending, marketing and exporting activities.

The progressive amalgamation of the Big Five with DCL

has already been described, as has the enormous part played by DCL in the Scotch whisky trade during the last fifty years. Today it is a vast concern, owning over forty distilling and blending firms,[24] forty-five of the just over one hundred malt distilleries now in operation and five of the ten grain distilleries, administered by its subsidiary company Scottish Grain Distillers Ltd. in the same way as its malt distilleries are administered by Scottish Malt Distillers Ltd. Finally, in the words of DCL's own publication, Scottish Grain Distillers Ltd. 'also produces, at Caledonian, Cambus, Carse-bridge and Port Dundas Distilleries, substantial quantities of carbon dioxide, in liquid and solid form, to meet the needs of the soft drinks, brewing and ice-cream industries, as well as for specialised use in foundry work and as a coolant by the Atomic Energy Authority'.

The growth and success of DCL is closely associated with the growth and success of blended Scotch whisky. And that in turn depended originally on Aeneas Coffey's invention of the patent still. Has the world-wide reputation of Scotch whisky been won at a cost? Are Aeneas Coffey, the great whisky *entrepreneurs* of the latter half of the nineteenth century and William Ross of DCL villains as much as heroes? There are some dedicated devotees of single malt whiskies who say that they are.

But this is to take a melodramatic and unrealistic view. The reputable blended Scotch whiskies are sound and pleasant drinks, if not as interesting, as individual or as flavoursome as a pure malt whisky. If – as Neil Gunn once maintained – the large drinking public on whom the Scotch whisky trade depends for its sales really prefer 'a tasteless alcohol' and go for the blended Scotch that approximates most closely to it, then in the long run Scotch will have to cede to vodka. But the evidence does not support Gunn's view, though it is true that in America there is a real demand for spirits of little characteristic flavour. Gunn's attack on the blenders was made in 1935, when the situation did indeed look desperate and the number of Highland malt distilleries at work was steadily diminishing. It looked, too, as though blending might do permanent injury to the production of the finer malts. 'If the pot-still product is too fine, too delicate,' wrote Gunn, 'in other words if it is a highly desirable single whisky, it will not communicate in sufficient measure to a waiting vat of patent spirit the characteristics of a Highland malt whisky; but, on the other hand, if it contains these characteristics in excessive degree, making it pungent and rather objectionable as a single whisky, it then achieves perfection for blending, on the principle that a little of it goes a long way.' But the situation described by Gunn has changed radically. The number and variety of pot-still malt distilleries now working and selling their product to the blenders makes it clear that there is no threat from the blenders to the finer malts. It is indeed quite wrong to suppose that the reputable blends today use a very little heavy and pungent malt whisky and avoid the lighter malts – the reverse is rather the truth. And the demand from the blenders for a range of good malt whiskies has been growing steadily. This is not to say that there is not a case against blended Scotch whisky, or at least against some blended Scotch whiskies. But before deciding on the merits of the issue we had better take a look at the nature and process of blending.

As I have already mentioned, and as anybody investigating the state of Scotch whisky today very quickly discovers, the Scotch whisky trade is unanimous in refusing to reveal the proportions of malt and grain whiskies that go into any given blend. While one can understand a refusal to reveal the precise nature and proportions of the different malts and grains that make up the blend, I have long felt that it is reasonable to expect to be told the proportions of malt and grain. Any given blend will still remain secret even if that information is released. One is indeed forced to suspect that a refusal to reveal these general proportions (which, to repeat, does not involve the revealing of the formula for the blend) is based on an underlying and perhaps subconscious desire to prevent the public from knowing that a large proportion of blended Scotch whisky is not pot-still malt whisky at all. In booklets and films blending houses will again and again explain and show in great detail the romantic, traditional process of making pot-still malt whisky; they have much less to say about patent-still grain whisky. Once, after seeing an advertising film on the production of Scotch whisky made for a distinguished blending house, and finding that it dealt exclusively with the making of pot-still Highland malt whisky, I rose from my place in the audience after the performance and asked the representative of the firm who was showing the film what proportion of the whisky in his firm's blend was actually made in that way, and why nothing had been shown of the making of patent-still whisky. It was not a question I was supposed to ask. It is true that the skill of the blender is played up enormously in whisky advertising; at the same time much of this advertising refers back to dates long before there was any blending of malt and grain whiskies. 'There are more than three centuries of affection and conviction behind our blend,' says an advertisement in an American magazine of Haig's 'pinch bottle'; 'established 1742' says the sign under the white horse and 'the white horse cellar' legend; an American advertisement of 'King William IV' whisky claims that it has been produced since 1817; and there is, of course, the famous 'Born 1820 – still going strong' slogan of 'Johnnie Walker'. My point is simply that in the advertising of blended whiskies the impression is given that the blends go back to dates long before blends existed and before the patent still was in fact invented. Further, how often do we find patent-still grain whisky mentioned in descriptions of blends? 'Rich Islay whiskies. Smooth whiskies from Falkirk and Campbeltown. Mellow Keith whisky, and the fragile whisky of Speyside.' That is from an American advertisement of '100 Pipers', a blend marketed by Seagrams, a relative newcomer to Scotland. Not a single patent-still grain whisky is mentioned. (The whisky from Falkirk is presumably Rosebank, a DCL Lowland malt distillery.) I could cite many other similar examples. It is almost as though the blenders are afraid to mention patent-still grain whisky. Of course, in the more technical information booklets issued by DCL and by the Scotch Whisky Association patent-still grain whisky is described (in as complimentary a way as possible). But in general the patent still is kept in the background.

So the blenders have only themselves to blame if one has to guess at the proportion of malt to grain in their whiskies. Of course, one's guesses can be helped out by other sources. Individuals in blending firms, while keeping quiet about the proportions in their own blend, will, on convivial occasions, risk a generalization about the proportions adopted in the trade generally. And one can use one's eyes. In visiting malt distilleries, for example, one can observe the colours of the ends of the casks in the warehouses : each blending house uses its own colour, so it is not difficult to see at a glance which blends use which malts. Indeed, managers of malt distilleries are not, in my experience, reluctant to tell you to what blenders they sell their whisky. But that is only part of the story. One may be able to form a pretty shrewd idea of the different malts in a blend without knowing what proportion of the blend is made up of malt whisky at all.

My own view is that in what one might call the standard blend of Scotch whisky today the proportion is 60 grain to 40 malt, and that the proportion of grain has risen since the earlier days of blending, when it was more likely to be 50 : 50.[25] I also believe that the 'light' whiskies being extensively pushed in the American market today (and increasingly in the home market too) are liable to have a significantly less proportion of malt than the 40 per cent of the standard blends. In the standard blends there is a basic distribution of malts, with Islays together with Eastern Malts of varying degrees of quality and maturity. Dewars claim that there are forty different whiskies in their blend; there are seventeen in the Glenlivet Distillers' 'Queen Anne' whisky. I have recently seen an advertisement for 'Johnnie Walker Black Label' claiming that 'over 40 Scotch whiskies' go into it. 'White Horse' claims 'thirty selected malt whiskies' in their blend. Some blends claim many more than this. I have no reason to question these claims, which are borne out by what one observes at distilleries. But nobody talks about the patent-still grain whiskies that make up the larger proportion of the blend. It is, further, the quality as well as the proportion of malt whisky in the blend that matters. There is no necessary gain in having an enormous range of malts if many of them are less mature or simply less good and the total proportion of malt remains small.

That there are inferior blends with a proportion of patent-still grain whisky of 80 per cent and even more can hardly be denied. But DCL's blends and those of well-known independent firms (some of which will be discussed later) are good and stable blends to which a great deal of careful thought has been given. Some independent firms produce superior blends which do not necessarily consist of a higher proportion of malts but may instead use more matured and better quality malts. This is also true of the higher priced 'quality' versions of some standard DCL blends, such as 'Johnnie Walker Black Label' or Dewar's 'Ancestor' (a whisky, incidentally, which is not advertised in Britain, because it is felt that the promoting of a superior Dewar blend might have adverse effects on the sales of their regular blend).

The actual blending process is not complicated. The whiskies to be blended, having been assembled from the various distilleries, are run through blending troughs (now often of stainless steel) into large vats. The whiskies in the blend can be 'roused' either by the modern method of running compressed air into the vats (as at the Dewar plant at Inveralmond) or by the older method of mechanical rousers. The blended whisky is then stored in oak casks for at least six months. Some blenders 'marry' the malts and the grains separately and bring them together only in bottling.

It is after blending and before bottling that artificial caramel colour is added. The blenders will tell you that this is to maintain evenness of colour, which the public expects. Whisky itself is colourless, and when matured in casks that have held sherry absorbs some of the sherry colour. But even if all whisky were matured in sherry casks (which is no longer so) the colour of each cask would be liable to come out differently. The public, it is argued, seeing one bottle of its favourite brand one day of a lighter colour than it had been before, will suspect the barman of watering it. The use of artificial colouring thus – the argument runs – reassures the public and maintains confidence.

I think this is nonsense, and contributes to the rubbish about whisky colour that is perpetuated in whisky advertising. The argument about the public's attitude could be disposed of very quickly : a six months' advertising campaign by the Scotch Whisky Association could educate the public as to the significance (or lack of significance) of colour in whisky and the campaign would be paid for by the saving in spectrometers, colorimeters and tintometers and their expert handlers which so many blending houses employ. I have seen a skilled tintometer operator carefully working out the amount of caramel colouring that goes into an eight-year-old (a very light colour this), a twelve-year-old (somewhat darker) and a twenty-year-old (darker still) blend, colouring the whisky according to its age[26] to fool the consumer into believing that the darker it is the older. They say that the sweet, gooey caramel stuff that goes into the whisky is in too insignificant proportions to affect the taste, but in the case of the darker coloured whiskies I am not so sure.[27]

Many of the blending firms now put less caramel colouring into their whisky that is exported to America because of the American mystique about lightness and paleness. This is a very odd thing. The American drinker seems to associate lightness in body, lightness in colour, and less likelihood of the consumer becoming intoxicated. Anyone who has drunk colourless 119° proof whisky straight from the still will know how ridiculous this is. But lightness is a powerful word in whisky advertising in the United States, and there is scarcely a Scotch whisky advertised there that doesn't use the word somewhere in the description of the whisky's quality. Some blenders have put on the market two versions of their whisky, one, sold as 'lighter', with less artificial colouring than the other, the only real difference being visual. I am told that this experiment has not gone well, and I confess that I am glad. If by a 'light' Scotch whisky one means a blended Scotch with a higher proportion of patent-still grain whisky in it, then in my view a 'light' Scotch is an inferior Scotch. If by a 'light' Scotch whisky one means a whisky light in colour, then the consumer who prefers this should be given a whisky matured in plain oak casks (which might be of any quality, any degree of body, and any strength). If by a 'light' Scotch whisky one means one of less alcoholic content, then it is a question of reducing proof and colour has nothing to do with the matter at all. My complaint is that the artificial colouring of Scotch whisky is unnecessary and misleading and also that the confusion of different kinds of lightness in whisky advertising misleads the public. Indeed I will go further and say that much whisky advertising, especially in the United States, the greatest single importer of Scotch whisky, is calculated to confuse the public as to what Scotch whisky is and how it can be recognized. By all means let people drink what they prefer; if they really want their whisky sharp and bodiless and not full and subtly flavoured let them have it that way; but don't fool them about the meaning of colour or tell them fairy stories about the ancient Scottish tradition of blending when you are selling them a whisky which bears very little relation to what Scotch whisky was before the development of blending in the latter part of the last century. As for 'lightness', the only use of the term that is at all helpful in discussing whisky refers to the kind of difference between, say, the delicate and fragrant Glenmorangie and the full-bodied, peaty Laphroaig – a difference, that is, in body and peatiness.

There is a further paradox involved in this business of lightness. One 'light' blend of Scotch is alleged to have been invented at the end of Prohibition to appeal to an American palate destroyed by bath-tub gin and similar monstrosities and totally incapable of appreciating the body and flavour of malt whisky. A blend of this kind, with a high proportion of patent-still grain whisky, is *sharp* both to the nose and to the palate. Yet lightness also seems to be aimed at the ladies, who are assumed by some manufacturers and advertisers to prefer a spirit as *bland* and tasteless as possible. Hence the present popularity in the United States of vodka and its use in a great variety of cocktails. American whisky, too, especially blended whisky, is increasingly presented as light and smooth (i.e. bland), which means with less definite taste and nose. But I repeat that some of the heavily advertised 'light' Scotches are not bland at all, but possess the sharpness that comes from the very high percentage of grain whisky. It is as though the sharpness is accepted as a guarantee that this really is an alcoholic spirit but that in all other respects the whisky is expected to be as tasteless, odourless, bodiless and even colourless as possible.

Incidentally, it is not only whisky that has been affected by popular myths about colour and lightness. Beer-drinking habits in England have been changing in accordance with the same beliefs. Mr J. A. P. Charrington, President of Bass Charrington, the large British brewing firm, discussed in a recent article the effect of increasing standardization of all kinds of consumer goods on changing tastes in beer as reflected by demand in English pubs. 'Beer is no exception to this overall standardization,' he wrote, 'and there is evidence that the public is moving from the highly hopped bitter beers to a smoother and blander palate. Young people particularly seem to prefer this kind of beer, and their popularity has been boosted by the strange belief that light coloured beers are alcoholically weaker and therefore safer with the breathalyzer[28] threat.' Mr Charrington also referred to the replacement of the traditional criterion of taste by the new criterion of stability and appearance in the customer's choice of beer. I suspect that this is happening over a wide variety of foods as well as drink; it seems to me to be a sad development.

Whisky matures in the cask and not in the bottle, and the kind of cask in which it matures is, of course, important. The practice of maturing malt whisky in sherry casks still goes on, though not universally : malt distilleries get sherry casks when they can and mature at least some of their whisky in them. The single whisky they bottle (those that do bottle their single malts) may be 'vatted' in the sense of made up of the same whisky, perhaps of different ages, matured in different casks, some sherry and some plain. Only recently I saw a noble collection of sherry butts (casks of 110 gallons) that had just arrived at Glenmorangie distillery, but not all Glenmorangie whisky is matured in sherry wood.

Sherry casks are used again and again, and repaired by the insertion of new sections from casks too far gone to be usable, so that there are casks in use which are partly original sherry casks and partly made from other casks or from new wood. There is thus a gradual and progressive introduction of new casks, with the new wood mixed in bit by bit and old casks being 'cannibalized'. In the cooperage at Dewar's huge plant at Inveralmond – as at other such plants and at numerous distilleries throughout Scotland – you can see the cooper at work in the old traditional way, repairing or re-building casks. Of course, there are also independent cooperage firms who supply the whisky distillers and blenders – Speyside Cooperage Ltd. of Craigellachie, for example, who manufacture new casks and repair sherry casks and refill casks for a great variety of distillers. Though distillers and blenders use sherry casks when they can, for at least a proportion of their maturing whisky, plain oak casks that have been 'wine treated' are increasingly used because the increased importing of sherry in containers is reducing the number of sherry casks available. 'Paxerette', a concentrated dark sweet sherry, is allowed to soak into the casks into which the maturing whisky will be put. But unless it is used in very small quantities the result can be unfortunate.

The best oak for maturing whisky is 'American white oak' (*Quercus alba*) from the United States. Many whisky casks are now imported direct from America. (Sherry casks, too, were often made from Arkansas oak and so came to Scotland from America via Spain: now they more and more come direct.) Casks that have held American bourbon whisky are imported in collapsed form and re-built with bigger ends into 55-gallon hogsheads. This is done for economic reasons: blenders own their casks which they send to particular distilleries for filling and may leave there for some to mature before taking delivery. They pay for the whisky at the time of filling, and then have to pay rent to the distillery for as long as they leave the whisky there. The rent is so much for each cask below 80-gallon capacity, so much for each cask above 80-gallon capacity. The scale of charges is such that rental on small casks proves un-economical. On the other hand, the bigger the cask the longer the period necessary for maturing, so the loss involved in having to wait a longer time till the whisky is ready must be balanced against the gain in having to pay a smaller rent.

Maturing is a less significant (and shorter) process for patent-still grain whisky: the most important part of the maturing process in a blended whisky is that which the malts in it have undergone before blending. Whisky once blended is kept at least six months in the cask (generally plain oak) to 'marry'. 'Vatted' whiskies – blended from malts of different distilleries – are now uncommon, but it is interesting that Dewars have recently put on the market a fine twelve-year-old 76° proof vatted malt whisky made up of matured malts they use for their luxury 'Ancestor' blend.

The proportion of single malts to blends consumed, even in Scotland, is very small; but there is nevertheless a steady rise in the availability and the consumption of single malts both in Britain and in certain overseas countries. I have seen a variety of single malt whiskies in a shop window in Venice, and in April 1975 I learned that a five-year-old Glen Grant was the best-selling whisky in Italy. At a large liquor super-market in Berkeley, California, I found some years ago, among an enormous variety of blended Scotch whiskies, both Glenlivet and Laphroaig (the former the twelve-year-old whisky bottled by the distillery in the familiar buff label), and the manager told me, somewhat to my surprise, that Laphroaig was the more popular, though the sales of neither compared to the sales of the blends. It was, inciden-tally, the same manager who told me that American whisky drinkers demanded a 'light' whisky but were confused as to whether this meant light in colour, light in body, or with less alcohol content. This was far from the first or the last time that I heard this.

Few single malt whiskies are advertised : they apparently make their way by verbal recommendation from the knowing to the less knowing. One occasionally sees them well displayed in the windows of wine merchants in Scotland : notable examples are Muirhead's in Edinburgh (owned by Macdonald and Muir, who own Glenmorangie and Glen Moray distilleries) and two Elgin wine and spirit merchants who themselves bottle a large number of malt whiskies – Gordon & Macphail and A. Campbell Hope and King, the former having a number of associated companies which export, blend, bond and distribute whisky. Some (but far from all) hotels in Scotland carry a wide range of single malts, though I must confess that some years ago when I asked what malts they had at the bar of a well-known hotel in Stirling, the barman told me that they only had Canadian Club ! I suspect that the situation has changed now. The Staff Club at Edinburgh University is famous for the range of single malts it carries. Glenfiddich is the only single malt Scotch whisky that has advertised consistently over a period of years; more recently Arthur Bell and Sons have been advertising their Dufftown and Blair Athol malt whiskies and their third malt, Inchgower, is also now available. I have found, in certain academic circles in America, an awareness and appreciation of single malts, and when dining recently with the distinguished American bibliographer Professor Fredson Bowers at Charlottesville, Virginia, I was offered a choice of Glenlivet and Talisker. As long ago as 1950, when I was teaching at Cornell University, I introduced American friends to Mortlach, available at Macy's in New York, and they took to it with enthusiasm. Perhaps the fact that it was matured in plain oak and was virtually colourless was held to be in its favour. I remember that I was asked to give a talk at the University on Scotch whisky, and in the course of my remarks I observed that one of the 'best buys' in pot-still Highland malt whisky was the

Mortlach available at Macy's. The next time I went to Macy's to re-stock for myself I was told that they were out of stock. When I expressed astonishment, the assistant said: 'Some damn fool professor at Cornell has been telling all his students to buy it, and we've run out.'

Single malt whiskies bottled and supplied in the United Kingdom by the DCL group are Aultmore, Cardhu, Clynelish, Glendullan, Lagavulin, Linkwood, Ord and Talisker, and also Rosebank, a Lowland malt. Some other of their malt whiskies are available in certain overseas markets. Among available single malt whiskies from distilleries outside the DCL group are Aberlour, Bowmore, The Glendronach (available in England since 1971), Glenlivet, Glen Grant, Glenfiddich, Glenmorangie, Glen Moray (since 1974) and Highland Park.

It has been suggested that there is a connection between the increased availability of single whiskies and the pushing of the 'lighter' blends with a greater proportion of grain; for the higher the proportion of grain whisky the less malt whisky will be used. As I have already mentioned, the blending firms will not themselves admit that these 'lighter' blends include a higher proportion of grain, though my own experience both in tasting and in talking to people working in blending firms is that the trend to a higher proportion of grain whisky in at least some blends is a real one. Anyway, we can at least observe what Cyril Ray has called the 'odd coincidence: the growing popularity of the whiskies at opposite ends of the scale of taste – the light blends that seem, at any rate, to incline more in character towards the grain whiskies, and the heavy unblended malts.'

So the 'self whisky' has survived the great international popularity of the blends and, in spite of some sticky moments, Aeneas Coffey's invention has not proved to be the end of the true pot-still malt whisky. It is not easy to predict the future. Some have seen the temptation 'to market blends of cheap grain whisky flavoured slightly with very young malt whisky' (in Professor McDowall's words) as a threat to the future of quality Scotches. The minimum age of three years (which many believe, as I do, ought to be increased to five) applies only to whisky sold on the home market, not to whisky exported, though if exported under three years old it must be described as spirit, not as whisky. There is a considerable export of fairly young whiskies in cask to America, where they are blended in some odd ways and given some odd names. Of course, many reputable blends are shipped to the USA in cask, which saves the Americans tax. And in spite of my objections to the way in which some blended whiskies are advertised, I can testify from my own knowledge to the integrity, efficiency and co-operativeness of DCL, whose distilleries are always clean and attractive and whole malt whiskies are produced in the traditional manner. Still, the expanding international consumption of Scotch whisky is bringing a great many new firms into the act, some of them more interested in selling their product than in maintaining quality. After all, the selling of Scotch whisky is one of the major businesses in the world, and I have myself spoken to people in the Scotch whisky trade (and not newcomers either) who seem willing to do pretty well anything to their whisky if they can produce it more cheaply and sell it in larger quantities. The danger of any alcoholic drink is that it can always be sold to those who simply want an alcoholic kick from it and have no interest in its quality and flavour.

Whisky, even if it is not Scotch whisky, is also being produced in increasing quantities in countries other than Scotland. Whether any other country will ever be able to produce a 'Scotch-type' whisky which is really comparable to genuine Scotch whisky in nature and quality remains doubtful. But if they don't it won't be for lack of trying. If such attempts outside Scotland are accompanied by a cutting of corners on the part of Scotch whisky distillers (speeding up and cheapening the process to produce less good whisky more easily) the future of Scotch whisky may well be in jeopardy. It is in the last analysis the great blending firms who determine what goes on in the whisky industry, and it is to be hoped that their sense of responsibility for maintaining quality will not be allowed to diminish. The only thing that the consumer can do in order to ensure that quality is maintained is to cultivate his palate, to learn to drink his Scotch whisky with true appreciation and discrimination. The scattered observations on different whiskies to be found in the next chapter are meant as one man's somewhat impressionistic contribution to that learning process.

7

Individual Distilleries

In this chapter I propose to say something more about individual distilleries and blending companies to show the situation as it is today. In chapter 2 I talked about the prestige of Glenlivet whisky even before George Smith decided to go legitimate in 1824. That prestige did not diminish after Smith's re-built and improved distillery began a new phase of its history. The distillery was at Upper Drumin, thirty-five miles partly over difficult country to the coast of the Moray Firth, and the whisky was sent by horse and cart to Garmouth and Burghead on the Firth whence it went south by boat. In 1863 the extension of the railway to Ballindalloch, about seven miles from the distillery, eased the transport problem somewhat. By this time Smith's son, Colonel John Gordon Smith, was in partnership with his father, and succeeded him on the latter's death at an advanced age in 1871. The Upper Drumin distillery had originally a capacity of only 50 gallons a week, which was increased to 200 gallons in 1839, but even this increase proved insufficient to meet the growing demand for Glenlivet. George Smith – who was an enterprising and pioneering farmer and cattle breeder as well as a distiller, and a great reclaimer of waste ground – had kept increasing the acreage he farmed, and in 1840 had taken the farm of Delnabo, above Tomintoul, where he had built another, smaller, distillery, the Cairngorm. But he and his son were still dissatisfied with their production of whisky : in 1858 they built a new and larger distillery on the farm of Minmore, which George Smith had first leased in 1840. The other two distilleries were scrapped, for the new Glenlivet distillery produced 600 gallons a week. Two new stills were put in in 1896 and the warehousing capacity has been much expanded since John Gordon Smith built four bonded warehouses in the 1860s. Until recently there were two still houses, each with one wash still and one spirit still, and ten wooden wash-backs. Although the Faemussach moss, with its great peat deposits, lies near the distillery, it has not done its own malting since 1966. Until 1972 the stills were heated by coal fires.

Such was the prestige of Glenlivet by the middle of the nineteenth century that other distilleries, not actually situated in Glenlivet but in that general part of Scotland, began to call themselves Glenlivet. It came to be said that Glenlivet was the longest glen in Scotland, so many distilleries were apparently situated there. In 1880 John Gordon Smith decided to go to law to protect the name of his whisky. The court's decision was that only Smith's Glenlivet was legally entitled to the name Glenlivet without any qualification. Other distilleries which used the name must hyphenate it with the true name of the particular distillery. Thus a large number of Eastern malt distilleries decided to hyphenate the word 'Glenlivet' with their name : Aberlour-Glenlivet, Aultmore-Glenlivet, Balmenach-Glenlivet, Balvenie-Glenlivet, Benromach-Glenlivet, Coleburn-Glenlivet, Convalmore - Glenlivet, Cragganmore - Glenlivet, Craigellachie-Glenlivet, Dailuaine-Glenlivet, Dufftown-Glenlivet, Glenburgie - Glenlivet, Glendullan - Glenlivet, Glen Elgin-Glenlivet, Glenfarclas-Glenlivet, Glen Grant-Glenlivet, Glen Keith-Glenlivet, Glenlossie-Glenlivet, Glen Moray-Glenlivet, Glenrothes-Glenlivet, Imperial-Glenlivet, Longmorn-Glenlivet, Macallan-Glenlivet, Miltonduff-Glenlivet, Speyburn-Glenlivet, Tamdhu-Glenlivet. These are fine whiskies, some of them splendid. DCL does not now use the name 'Glenlivet' in the titles of any of its distilleries, and this makes sense, since none in the above list really needs this designation to prove its merit. The only whisky which can call itself 'The Glenlivet', or just 'Glenlivet', is 'Smith's Glenlivet'.

Only 5 per cent of Glenlivet is today bottled as a single whisky : the rest goes to the blenders, and all the important blenders except Teacher's take some Glenlivet. The distillery itself bottles (though not at the distillery) only a twelve-year-old, which is splendid, though I have tasted admirable older

Glenlivets bottled by Berry Bros. & Rudd. Other bottlers bottle it at different ages: Gordon & MacPhail of Elgin bottle a variety of ages, each with a differently coloured label. If I had to single out one classic of malt whiskies it would be the twelve-year-old Glenlivet.

But to return to the history of Glenlivet. John Gordon Smith died in 1901 and was succeeded by his nephew, Colonel George Smith Grant, son of Margaret Smith (who was the daughter of the original George Smith) and William Grant. Colonel Smith Grant kept up the Glenlivet tradition of farming as well as distilling. He was a great stock breeder, and had a notable Aberdeen-Angus herd. He was succeeded in 1918 by his younger son William Henry Smith Grant, after the death in the war in May of that year of his elder son John Gordon Smith Grant. In March 1951 the firm became a private company with Captain William Smith Grant as Chairman and in 1952 it joined with another distinguished distilling firm, J. & J. Grant, Glen Grant Ltd., to form a public company, The Glenlivet & Glen Grant Distilleries Ltd.

In 1972 the hitherto independent blending firm of Hill Thomson merged with the Glenlivet and Glen Grant Distilleries to form The Glenlivet Distilleries Ltd. Glenlivet Distillery has seen many changes in recent years. They now have three pairs of stills (three wash stills, three spirit stills) in the same building and in 1972 they introduced gas (LPG) firing. Nothing, however, is changed in the actual method of distilling. There has been no speeding up, even though this would be possible with gas heating, for this might affect the quality of the whisky. They built a new mash house in 1972 and a new still house in 1973. Their new mash tuns are all covered (this is becoming standard practice in distilleries), and this keeps everything cleaner. Three mashes are produced every twenty-four hours. They have three double-size wash-backs, each holding 14,200 gallons. They now use condensers instead of the traditional worm-and-tub for cooling, which is much more efficient and is also becoming more and more common in distilleries. There has been no cut-back in production. The distillery works 168 hours a week, with a staggered shut-down for cleaning. The gas firing of the stills means that one man now looks after six stills whereas previously two men looked after four. Automatic controls make the work lighter and more precise, thus increasing rather than threatening the effectiveness of the traditional mode of distilling.

Glen Grant distillery was founded by John and James Grant who in 1840 moved their distillery from Dandaleith, where they had been distilling whisky since 1834, two and a half miles north to Rothes (between Craigellachie and Elgin). Legend has it that well before 1834 they were whisky smugglers in Glenlivet. But we do know for certain that James Grant, who may well have known George Smith, studied law in Edinburgh and in 1829, at the age of twenty-eight, set up as a solicitor in Elgin. But law did not satisfy him, and he moved to a number of other activities including distilling. By March 1842 a writer in *The Second Statistical Account of Scotland* was able to talk about 'one of the most extensive distilleries in the North . . . established in Rothes by Messrs J. and J. Grant, in which establishment between 30,000 and 40,000 gallons of whisky are annually made'. With the distillery producing 1500 gallons of whisky a week it is not surprising that James Grant became interested in railways : transport has always been a problem for Highland malt distillers. He worked hard and successfully to get a railway laid between Lossiemouth and Elgin and between Elgin and Rothes, and served as Provost of Elgin for fifteen years. James Grant was succeeded in 1872 by his son, Major James Grant, who died in 1931 at the age of eighty-three and was succeeded by his grandson, Mr Douglas Mackessack, who is now managing director of both Glen Grant and Caperdonich distilleries.

Glen Grant distillery at Rothes was considerably enlarged in 1865, seven years before James Grant's death. In 1897 Major James Grant built a second distillery. At the insistence of the excise authorities, the whisky from the new distillery had to be pumped to the original distillery, where the two whiskies were mixed. The whisky was pumped through a pipe which crossed the main street of Rothes and was known locally as the 'Whisky Pipe'. But the end of the whisky boom which followed the Pattison failure in 1898 made it increasingly difficult to keep the new distillery going, and it had to close down in 1901. However, the steady expansion of whisky exports which has led to the present prosperity of the whisky industry led Grants to re-open the second distillery in 1965. It is now called Caperdonich distillery and was completely modernized in 1967. Before 1967 it operated with its two original stills, one wash still and one spirit still. Now it has two new stills (one wash still and one spirit still) heated by steam coils, and it also has a remarkable system of automatic controls. Any process can now be operated by button-pushing from a central position. The grinding of a specific quantity of malt, the charging or discharging of the stills, the starting of conveyors and the opening of elevators – all this can be done from a central control. Neither Glen Grant nor Caperdonich now does its own malting; they buy their malt ready dried from Robert Hutchison & Co. Ltd. of Kirkcaldy and other suppliers. This is increasingly the practice with distillers.

Caperdonich distillery and Glen Grant distillery use water from the same burn, but, of course, the two whiskies are not identical. A five-year-old Caperdonich was sold in Italy for a short period, to supplement the five-year-old Glen Grant for which the demand exceeded the supply, but when Hill Thomson were absorbed in Glenlivet Distilleries they wanted it all for their luxury blend 'Something Special' and so none was left for bottling as a single whisky. Most of Glen Grant, too – at least 95 per cent – goes to the blenders; as with Glenlivet it is taken by virtually every one of the important blenders. But fortunately, again as with Glenlivet, it is also available as a single whisky. A variety of ages are available; I should say that the fifteen-year-old shows the whisky at its best, but the ten-year-old is a fine whisky and the eight-year-old is eminently drinkable. The Glen Grant label, by the way, has remained unchanged for generations : it is a splendid example of Victorian design.

Glen Grant distillery has a new still house, with two new

stills and space for four more. Four stills are coal fired; the two new ones are fired by LPG gas. There has been an increase of 63 per cent over the capacity of the original two coal-fired stills, with a projected increase of 163 per cent when the four new stills are finally introduced. There are four new wash-backs.

There are about fifty Highland malt distilleries situated near enough to the Spey valley for their product to be considered Speyside whisky. Many of these, as we have seen, hyphenate 'Glenlivet' to their name. In spite of common features possessed by all Speyside whiskies, each has its own distinctive quality : some are discussed below. Each distillery, too, has its characteristic customs and methods, though all use the traditional pot-still process. Many have been modernized in recent years, but new stills have always scrupulously copied the shape of the old. The small but numerous low wines stills of Glenfiddich distillery, for example, strike the observer's eye : on one side there are five low wines stills of 1100 gallons capacity and two wash stills of 2000 gallons, and on the other side three low wines stills and two wash stills. Glenfiddich is one of the growing number of distilleries that buy their malt. Mortlach distillery, Dufftown, buy about two-thirds of the malt they need and do their own malting for the remaining third : here there are three wash stills and three low wines stills, one of the wash stills being of 4200 gallons and the other stills being of varying sizes from 1800 to 2350 gallons. Mortlach uses the traditional coal fires under the stills, as many Highland malt distilleries still do. Longmorn, the distillery near Elgin that was founded in 1894, for long used coal fires. Its four wash stills are still fired by solid fuel but its four spirit stills are now heated by steam cones (not coils), which give a very fine control. Of the eight stills, three use worm tubs for cooling and five use condensers. Longmorn still does some of its own malting, but this represents a small proportion of the malt it uses. Its new wash tuns are covered, as at Glenlivet. Altogether Longmorn, with its recently increased capacity and new automatic controls, gives the impression of a distillery that faces the future with complete confidence. It has more than doubled its production of whisky in recent years. Its sister distillery of Benriach, almost next door, which was re-opened in 1965 after a long period of idleness, uses steam coils. (Both these distilleries are now owned by Glenlivet Distilleries Ltd.) Benriach now produces a light-bodied malt whisky, which goes entirely for blending. Some stillmen claim that coal fires have something to do with the quality of the whisky produced, others do not think so. In the bright modern distillery of Tormore, where the eight wash-backs are of steel and are cleaned by an automatic device known as 'Sputnik', their four stills (two wash stills of 4050 gallons capacity and two low wines stills of 3000 gallons) are heated by coal fires, automatically stoked.

One could pick out examples of varying practices and varying beliefs from a great range of Highland malt distilleries. To look farther north than Speyside, Glenmorangie distillery has unusually high stills – both the wash stills and the low wines stills are of the same height, the former of 3500 gallons capacity and the latter of 2000 gallons – and they attribute the quality of the whisky partly to the height of the stills, which have long been heated by steam coils. In some distilleries the low wines stills are distinctly smaller and of a slightly different shape from that of the wash stills; in others they are about the same. In Lagavulin distillery, Islay, there are two wash stills of 4146 gallons capacity each : they are approximately the same shape, but the wash stills are a bit narrower and longer at the top. Lagavulin does most of its own malting, and uses mostly southern English barley (from East Anglia). They do, however, buy in some extra malt as they find they cannot make enough themselves. The stills are heated by coal fires. In nearby Laphroaig distillery the stills are heated by steam coils; there are two wash stills of 2000 gallons capacity each and three low wines stills of 800 gallons. They also do their own malting, and the last time I was there they were using Australian barley. Laphroaig is the only distillery in Scotland with a woman as chairman – Mrs Wishart Campbell, who combines a brisk efficiency with charm.

One could go on rambling round the malt distilleries, picking out characteristics of each, but enough has probably been said to give some idea of their differences as well as their common features. Of the ninety-five Highland malt distilleries (including eight in Islay and two in Campbeltown) now operating, forty-two are in the DCL group and are operated by Scottish Malt Distillers Ltd. Of the ten Lowland malt distilleries now functioning, DCL through SMD operate three (Glenkinchie, Rosebank and St Magdalene). Among the DCL Highland malt distilleries are twenty in the Speyside area (Aultmore, Benrinnes, Benromach, Balmenach, Cardow, Coleburn, Convalmore, Cragganmore, Craigellachie, Dailuaine, Dallas Dhu, Glendullan, Glen Elgin, Glenlossie, Glentauchers, Imperial, Knockdhu, Linkwood, Mortlach and Speyburn), two in the Moray Firth area (Banff and Royal Brackla), three near the east coast (Brechin, Glenury and Hillside), one on Deeside (Royal Lochnagar), two in Central Scotland (Dalwhinnie and Aberfeldy), one in Inverness (Millburn) one not far away at Beauly (Ord), one at Fort William (Glenlochy), one at Oban (Oban), one on the Cromarty Firth (Teaninich), and two (Clynelish and Brora) in Sutherland. In 1972, by buying complete control of Mackinlays & Birnie, DCL acquired Glen Albyn and Glen Mhor distilleries. The Islay distilleries of Caol Ila, Lagavulin and Port Ellen are also in the DCL group, as is Talisker, on the Isle of Skye. Five distilleries are owned by the Highland Distilleries Company, Limited, a company which dates back to 1887. They are the Islay distillery of Bunnahabhain, Glen Rothes-Glenlivet, Tamdhu-Glenlivet, and Highland Park, the last being one of the Orkney distilleries of which the other is Scapa, acquired by Hiram Walker in 1965 and run by Taylor & Ferguson. The ownership of the other Highland malt distilleries is indicated in the accounts of the rise of the various blending companies either above in chapter 4 or below in this chapter. Some are still family businesses or run by private limited companies. Macallan-Glenlivet (it is now dropping the 'Glenlivet' from its label) is owned by R. Kemp-Macallan-Glenlivet Ltd.; Glenfarclas-Glenlivet is

well thought of. There are other blending houses with excellent reputations within the DCL group; my present purpose, however, is not to provide a catalogue of all such firms but merely to give some idea of their range and variety.

The range of DCL blended Scotch whiskies is wide, from the full-flavoured 'White Horse' with its discernible Islay component to the sweeter, less peaty 'Vat 69'. In the middle of this spectrum I would place Dewar's,[80] a sound blend leaning neither to smokiness on the one hand nor sweetness on the other, together with 'Black and White' and 'Johnnie Walker'. 'Haig' has a bit more fullness than these : Professor McDowall has spoken of its 'delicious after-flavour which lingers on the palate', but, while I find it a thoroughly agreeable blend, I cannot say that I myself have been struck by this after-taste. Which goes to show the extraordinarily personal quality of whisky appreciation. Not only do some drinkers prefer a flavour which others positively dislike (the distinctive flavour of 'White Horse', for example, makes it a whisky which people who really taste the whisky they drink either insist on or avoid), but some actually taste or smell elements which others cannot discover at all. I have already declared my interest : I am normally a drinker of single pot-still malt whiskies, though there are a considerable number of blends which I drink with pleasure in the appropriate circumstances.

All of the DCL blended Scotch whiskies are conscientiously produced blends of good quality, but this does not mean that some independent firms do not produce admirable blends. Matthew Gloag and Son of Perth, a small but long-established firm which was bought by Highland Distilleries in 1970, produce in their 'Famous Grouse' whisky a very fine blend, full and round, containing an unusually high proportion of matured malts. Personally, I would put 'Famous Grouse' whisky very near the top of my list of blended Scotches. There are also larger and more widely known firms outside the DCL group who produce fine blends. I can discuss only a few of these, but would emphasize that this book makes no claim to provide a full list of producers of good blended Scotch whisky : there is bound to be an element of arbitrariness in the selection I mention.

One of the oldest as well as one of the largest independent Scotch whisky firms is that of Arthur Bell & Sons Ltd., whose history begins in Perth in 1825. In that year a distiller named T. R. Sandeman opened a shop on the south side of the ancient church of St John and began to trade as a whisky-merchant. Some years later the business was operated by James Roy and shortly before the middle of the nineteenth century it was known as Roy and Miller. Arthur Bell joined the firm in 1851 and for a time it was known as Roy and Bell. It was Bell and Sandeman between 1862 and 1865, in which year Arthur Bell took over sole control. In 1895 he was joined by his two sons, Arthur Kinmond Bell and Robert Bell, and the firm assumed the name of Arthur Bell & Sons. Bell's became a limited company in 1922, shortly after opening its present head-quarters in Victoria Street, Perth. A. K. Bell (widely known as 'A. K.') became Chairman and Managing Director of the limited company : the original Arthur Bell had died in 1900. 'A. K.' was a notable figure in Perth, and is remembered for his establishment of the Gannochy Trust which has done so much for the amenities of the city. There is now no longer a Bell among the company's directors. The present Chairman and Managing Director is Mr W. G. Farquharson, who took over on A. K. Bell's death in 1942.

The firm was not, of course, originally a blending firm. It purchased pot-still malt whisky from farmer-distillers and stored it in its warehouses in Perth before sale. It was the blending boom of the last three decades of the nineteenth century that brought Bell's into blending, at first on a small scale, buying whiskies from different distilleries. In 1933, during a period of depression for Scotch whisky, when many distilleries found it hard or impossible to carry on, Bell's bought the Blair Athol distillery, Pitlochry, and the Dufftown-Glenlivet distillery, Dufftown, and in 1936 they bought Inchgower distillery (near Buckie on the Moray Firth). In the eighteenth century the area around Pitlochry had been noted for illegal distilling, and Blair Athol distillery, taking advantage, like George Smith of Glenlivet, of the new Act of 1823, 'went legitimate' in 1825. Inchgower distillery had been built in 1871 and Dufftown in 1887.

Bell's still maintains its head office in Perth. They have bonded warehouses at Perth, Edinburgh, Halbeath (near Dunfermline, Fife) and Auchtermuchty (Fife). In 1967 they opened a £1,000,000 bottling and blending plant on an eighteen-acre site at East Mains Industrial Estate near Broxburn, West Lothian. This includes a huge bottling hall with six loading tables and provision for an additional three to be installed later. The bottling is automatic, with an electronic console controlling the flow of whisky to each bottling line. Some blending is still done at the firm's older premises at Leith.

Bell's advertising slogan is 'Afore ye go', which appears at the base of the neck of each bottle. It is the largest selling whisky in Scotland, fairly light in body, slightly sharp to the nose, but with an agreeable after-taste of Eastern malts. Bell's has 11% of the total United Kingdom Scotch whisky market, coming equal with Teacher's Highland Cream after Haig (15%) and Johnnie Walker (12%).

Another old-established blended whisky outside the DCL group is 'Long John', with a history also going back to 1825, when John Macdonald, known as Long John because of his great height, took advantage of the 1823 Act and built Ben Nevis distillery at Fort William. Long John died in 1856, and his son took over the distillery. But the firm did not remain in the Macdonald family. The name 'Long John' was sold in 1911 to W. H. Chaplin & Co. Ltd., London wine and spirit merchants, by which time the whisky was no longer the Highland malt whisky it had originally been, but a blend. In 1935 Long John Distilleries Ltd., as the firm had by now become, was taken over by Seager Evans, originally established in 1805 as gin distillers in London. Long John had in 1927 built the Strathclyde distillery in Glasgow, a patent-still grain distillery, and in 1937 the firm acquired the Highland malt distillery of Glenugie, near Peterhead, which had been built in 1875. In 1956 Seager Evans was bought by Schenley Industries

Inc. of the United States. Schenleys brought new capital and vigorous new expansion into the production of 'Long John'. Mr John Mackie, a Scot who had spent twelve years working with Canadian Schenley Ltd., returned to his native country to be chairman of Seager Evans and to pursue the policy of expansion. In 1957 Long John Distilleries built the Lowland malt distillery of Kinclaith near Glasgow and in 1958–9 built their splendid new Tormore distillery, designed by Sir Albert Richardson, past President of the Royal Academy. Tormore is now one of the show malt distilleries on Speyside, and has recently bottled its own eight-year-old single malt whisky. At the same time Long John has enormously expanded its warehousing facilities and is planning as a long-term project a great new complex of distilleries, warehouses, and bottling plant at Westthorn Farm, Glasgow, where they already have a warehousing and blending depot and where the building of a great new bottling plant has already commenced. It is some time since I have tasted 'Long John', but I remember it as a whisky somewhere in the middle of the spectrum, lacking that metallic taste which I sometimes detect in blends.

Seager Evans and Co. changed its name to Long John International in 1971. They have available for their 'Long John' whisky two Highland malt distilleries (Tormore and Glenugie), a Lowland malt distillery at Kinclaith and a grain whisky distillery at Strathclyde. In addition, they have the distinguished Islay distillery of Laphroaig, run by the Johnston family from 1815 to 1954 and owned by D. Johnston & Co. Ltd. since 1950 : in 1962 D. Johnston & Co. merged with Seager Evans. The story of 'Long John' whisky thus involves a pattern of amalgamation and expansion reminiscent of that of DCL itself. Long John Distilleries Ltd. still exist as a working entity, and the name will be found on bottles of 'Long John' and of Tormore. Laphroaig is bottled under the label 'D. Johnston & Co. (Laphroaig) Ltd.', as is 'Islay Mist', a blend of Laphroaig and other whiskies. Long John International also put out 'Black Bottle', a blend, through Gordon Graham & Co. of Aberdeen.

Another important independent firm is William Grant & Sons Ltd., whose brand name 'Standfast' (from the Grant clan battle cry, 'Stand Fast!') is over seventy-five years old. The original William Grant of Glenfiddich worked for some years in Mortlach distillery before building Glenfiddich distillery, which began operations in 1887. It is said that the first salesman for Grant's whisky made 500 calls before he sold a case; but they have come a long way since then. The firm built Balvenie distillery, Dufftown, in 1871, and in 1955 greatly enlarged their original Glenfiddich distillery. In 1962 they opened a £1,250,000 grain distillery at Girvan, Ayrshire, and a vast blending and bottling plant at Paisley, with four automatic bottling lines. They have also recently opened Ladyburn Lowland malt distillery at Girvan. 'Standfast' is one of the notable blends, and is exported to 154 countries as well as enjoying a comfortable share of the home market. Grant's also bottle their Glenfiddich as a straight malt whisky, the first straight malt to be publicized in a national advertising campaign. In 1973 they put their other single malt whisky, 'Balvenie', on the market. Both are characteristic eastern malts, 'Glenfiddich' slightly the less peaty of the two but both are light on peatiness. I personally prefer either of these malts to 'Standfast', but the latter is a well-balanced blend of distinctive character.

An Edinburgh blending firm whose history goes back to 1793 is Hill Thomson & Co. Ltd., now a part of the Glenlivet Distillers Ltd. Their 'Queen Anne' whisky is well known. William Hill set up business as a wine and spirit merchant in Rose Street Lane (behind Princes Street) in 1793, and six years later moved to 45 Frederick Street, an elegant Georgian house where the firm still has its head office. On William Hill's death in 1818 his two sons continued the business under the name of Messrs William and Robert Hill; but they both died relatively young and a third brother George took control of the business on Robert's death in 1837. William Thomson was taken into partnership in 1857 and the firm became Hill Thomson & Co. It was William Shaw, an energetic young man who entered the business in 1883, who produced the blend 'Queen Anne' and developed the export trade. Since then the Shaw family have been prominent in the firm. William Shaw's sons, W. D. and J. N. Shaw, became partners in 1919, and in 1936, six years after their father's death, formed a limited company, Hill Thomson & Co. Ltd., with themselves as joint managing directors. Since then sales have been further developed abroad, notably in Europe, the Middle and Far East, and South Africa. In addition to 'Queen Anne' (a distinctive blend with a predominantly Speyside after-taste), the firm produces an extra quality whisky, 'Something Special', and they export two other of their blends, 'Hilltop' and 'St Leger'. They also bottle an 83° proof gin (94.8° American proof), 'Old Gentry'.

The firm of W. and A. Gilbey represents a different pattern of growth. Walter and Alfred Gilbey set up as wine-merchants in London in 1857 and then went into the distillation of gin. The ravages of phylloxera in the French vineyards in the 1880s led them to expand into the whisky trade : in 1887 they bought Glen Spey distillery, Rothes, and in 1904 Knockando distillery, Cardow, both of which Highland malt distilleries the firm still owns in addition to Strathmill distillery, Keith. They went in only for malt whisky at first, but the blending boom proved irresistible : Gilbey's 'Spey Royal' has long been an established blend with a distinct Speyside malt flavour. In 1962 Gilbey's merged with International Distillers and Vintners, among whose constituent companies was the old-established firm of London wine-merchants Justerini and Brooks (hence 'J. & B. Rare' blended Scotch whisky). In 1972 International Distillers and Vintners was bought by the brewery firm of Watney Mann, which was then in turn taken over by Grand Metropolitan Hotels. This is now a large empire which includes Dominic's, the chain of retail wine and spirit merchants.

A firm which is increasingly coming into public notice is Whyte & Mackay Ltd., 'an independent company established 1844' as their advertising used to claim, though James Whyte and Charles Mackay did not enter on their partnership until 1882. In that year they took over the firm of Allan and Paynter, which certainly does go back to 1844. They produce three blends, their 'Special', which they rightly describe as 'one of the oldest proprietary brands' since it dates from the beginning of the Whyte and Mackay partnership; 'Supreme', a fuller whisky with a higher proportion of malts; and '21 Years Old'. Whyte & Mackay merged in 1960 with Mackenzie Brothers, proprietors of Dalmore distillery, Ross-shire, a Highland malt distillery which goes back to 1839 and with which the Mackenzie family have been associated since 1867. In 1972 Dalmore Whyte & Mackay were taken over by Scottish & Universal Investments.

One of my favourite pot-still malt whiskies is 'Glenmorangie', produced at Glenmorangie Distillery, Tain, which is one of two distilleries (the other is Glen Moray, north of Elgin, whose single malt whisky was made available in 1973) owned by Macdonald & Muir Ltd., whisky blenders of Queen's Dock, Leith. 'Glenmorangie' has become increasingly popular, in England as well as Scotland, and the assignment of its distribution in England and Wales to Dent & Reuss Ltd. (the wines and spirits subsidiary of the cider firm of Bulmer) in July 1974 made it more readily available. Macdonald & Muir began in 1893; their blend is 'Highland Queen', which contains 'Glenmorangie' among other whiskies, and they also produce a fifteen-year-old blend, 'Grand 15'. Macdonald & Muir also blend and export 'Martin's VVO' of three different ages, eight, twelve and twenty years old; other of their whiskies, perhaps less well known, are Muirhead's (Gold Label, Silver Label, and 'Rare Old Maturity' twelve years old) and 'Glen Moray '93', a de luxe whisky described with engaging *bravura* as 'of tremendous stature, yet full of grace'. (This description comes from the wine list of Charles Muirhead & Sons Ltd., an attractive Edinburgh retail firm owned by Macdonald & Muir. It is so far as I know the only place in the United Kingdom where 'Martin's VVO', virtually unobtainable in Britain because it is blended almost entirely for export, can sometimes be bought.)

I must emphasize again that in this section of the book

I am picking out a number of firms representing different types and categories and not making any attempt to cover the whole field or even to discuss a substantial selection. There are many good blends that are not mentioned here. But I cannot conclude this account of some different types of blending houses outside the DCL group without saying a word about that well-known blend 'Teacher's Highland Cream', produced by a firm which goes back to 1830 and remained in the family until 1923. Since 1949 the firm has been Teachers (Distillers) Ltd. The name 'Highland Cream' was first used in 1884, and the blend was originally based on malt whisky from Ardmore distillery, Kennethmont, Aberdeenshire, which William Teacher built in 1891 and which the firm still owns. In 1962 the firm acquired Glendronach distillery, originally built in 1826; in the same year they built a great new blending and bottling plant in Craig Park, Glasgow.

I must mention, too, the two important Canadian firms who have entered the Scotch whisky field. Hiram Walker of Ontario first acquired interests in Scottish bonding and distilling companies in the early 1930s, and followed this up by acquiring George Ballantine & Sons of Dumbarton and the Miltonduff-Glenlivet distillery near Elgin. They had already taken over the firm of James & George Stodart Ltd., owners of Glenburgie-Glenlivet distillery, Forres, Morayshire. In 1955 they acquired another Stodart distillery, Pulteney distillery in Wick, whose admirable 'Old Pulteney' malt whisky is discussed below. By this time they also had their own Lowland malt distillery of Inverleven, Dumbarton, and went on to build a great grain distillery also at Dumbarton. They also acquired Glencadam distillery, Brechin, and Scapa distillery, Kirkwall, Orkney, both in 1954. They have a large blending and bottling plant at Dumbarton, where they also now have a second Lowland malt distillery, Lomond. (This is not the same as Loch Lomond distillery, the highly automated Highland malt distillery owned by the Littlemill Distillery Co. Ltd. and opened in 1966.) Hiram Walker (Scotland) Ltd., with its numerous distilleries and its facilities for blending and warehousing, is thus in a position to put out a great variety of blended Scotch whiskies, though none bears the name of Hiram Walker. It is in fact (like DCL) a group of associated companies which, though under the general umbrella of Hiram Walker, maintain their identity and compete with each other. 'Ballantine's' is probably the best known of the blends put out by the Walker group and is highly esteemed among connoisseurs of blends; among the nineteen others are 'Old Smuggler' (which I have seen a great deal in the United States), 'Ambassador' (a de luxe blend) and 'Thorne's' (also well known in America).

The other Canadian firm that has come to Scotland is Seagrams. In 1928 Samuel Bronfman,[31] who had already developed his own distilling company in Montreal, bought the Canadian firm of Joseph Seagram & Sons, and later became president of the giant Distillers-Seagrams Ltd. Seagrams is a well-known Canadian rye whisky. But Mr Bronfman also had a nose for Scotch, and in 1950 he took over the old-established Aberdeen firm of Chivas Brothers. In the same year Chivas acquired the distillery of Milton, Keith, changing its name to Strathisla-Glenlivet. Under Mr Bronfman's control – he took a great personal interest in this – Chivas developed, with their Strathisla-Glenlivet and other whiskies, their rich and mellow luxury blend, 'Chivas Regal'. Seagrams also built the Glen Keith-Glenlivet distillery, on the other side of the town from Strathisla, so Chivas now have these two malt distilleries in Keith. Seagrams have also developed a number of other blends of Scotch whisky, including '100 Pipers' and 'Passport'.

Sam Bronfman died in 1971 and was succeeded by his son Edgar. The firm, which changed its name to The Seagram Co. Ltd. in 1974, claims to be the 'world's largest liquor company'. In December 1974 Mr Edgar Bronfman announced an investment of £14m. in expanding its Scotch whisky interests. With its enormous stocks of mature and maturing whisky, the DCL group can afford to cut distillation of new whisky in the immediate future, but Seagrams, which only seriously came into the Scotch whisky scene in the 1950s, needs to build up its stocks to cope with the expansion of its brands. Seagrams also sends Scottish malt whisky to its new distillery in Japan, which it jointly owns with the Kirin brewing group. There it is blended with local grain spirit to make Japanese whisky.

8

Individual Whiskies

Knowledge about the equipment of distilleries and the history of blending firms is no necessary help to discriminating drinking. How should whisky be drunk? Is it a crime to drink it with soda, ginger ale or lemonade? Are whisky cocktails indecencies? How old should whisky be before it can be properly enjoyed? Is it mere snobbery to prefer a single malt whisky to a blend?

The first thing to be said about the drinking of whisky is that all traditions, customs, fashions, rules and snobberies which do not help a given individual to enjoy his whisky are so much nonsense as far as that individual is concerned. The rule is simple: what you enjoy best is best. The real question is whether what you casually or lazily think you enjoy best is what you really do enjoy best or would enjoy best if you experimented more widely and paid more attention to what you drink when you drink it. The trouble with any alcoholic drink is that it can be drunk by people who dislike the taste and who are simply out for the alcoholic kick. It used to be standard practice in Hollywood films for actors to indicate when they were taking an alcoholic drink by the grimacing gulp which accompanied its rapid ingestion, the implication clearly being that it tastes horrible but you drink it for social reasons or because it makes you feel good. There are, of course, social reasons for drinking whisky, and it does enhance your sense of well-being, but the main reason for drinking whisky rather than any other form of spirit is (or so it seems to me) its taste and flavour. That is one reason why I am prejudiced against those 'lighter' blends which seem to be designed to please the palate of those who do not like the characteristic taste of Scotch whisky. Rather than serve up as Scotch whisky a blend so made up that it has lost most of the aroma, flavour and body that really distinguishes Scotch whisky from other potable spirits, I would have such blends marketed under a quite different name. There is nothing improper in people preferring these blends; but surely people ought to be helped to know what to look for as characteristic qualities of the spirit traditionally and uniquely distilled in Scotland.

Having said this, I go on to announce my tolerance. Do Americans like a Scotch 'highball' in a tall glass with soda and lots of ice? Scotch and soda, with or without ice, is an excellent hot-weather drink, and I enjoy it myself under the proper conditions. And if I were drinking Scotch and soda I would certainly drink a good blend and not a single whisky. I find that the grainy[32] taste that comes, as it were, off the surface of a blended Scotch whisky if drunk straight, is either lost when the whisky is mixed with soda or combines with the effervescence of the soda in a way that satisfies the desire for a refreshing long drink. That grainy taste, by the way, I find in almost all blends as a first, surface flavour; the malt in the blend comes out as an after-taste – indeed, one of the best ways to distinguish between blends is to 'listen' for that after-taste, and even assist it by letting the flavour out of your nose just after you have swallowed. It is logical that blended Scotch whisky should have been developed largely for English palates used to brandy and soda. Under the right temperature conditions, I consider the traditional Scotch and soda an excellent drink.

But it would be a mistake to add soda to a single malt whisky. Any whisky, single malt or blended, can be savoured neat or with plain water, but with a single malt neat and with plain water are the only alternatives. And no ice. The reason for this can easily be demonstrated by anyone for himself. Ice sharply diminishes the availability of all the subtle flavours in a malt whisky that are provided by the 'congenerics'. Soda, too, kills much of the characteristic flavour of a malt whisky, or at least disperses it in an intolerable way. If whisky is to be diluted, it is best of all to dilute both malt and blended whisky with the local water that is used either in making it or in reducing it for maturing. I have drunk twelve-year-old Glenlivet at the distillery qualified with the water from the local wells where they get the water they use in making the whisky, and there is no doubt that it tastes better than the same whisky drunk with just any old water. I have proved this again and again while 'taking a dram' in a distillery manager's office. This goes for blended whisky too. When I drank Dewar's at their Inveralmond plant qualified with water from Loch Ordie which they use in reducing the strength of the whiskies they receive at about 117° proof from the distilleries, it tasted better than the same whisky mixed with tap water. Of course, a lot depends on which tap water it is. Water has taste, and some household water supplies are chlorinated (sometimes, in America, very heavily) or may have any of a great variety of flavours from a great variety of sources. This is why, for diluting blended whisky, there is a good case for preferring soda to water unless the water is spring water or from some other known and approved source. I myself, when I am not lucky enough to be drinking whisky at the distillery with the same water the distillery uses in making it, dilute my whisky (when I do dilute it) with Schweppes Malvern water.

As we have seen, whisky is reduced to 70° proof (for the home market) before bottling, and one might think that it made no difference to the taste whether one drank it from the bottle at 70° proof or got it at a much higher proof at the distillery and diluted it to 70° or so in the glass at the time of drinking. But the fact is that it tastes better in the latter case. Time and again I have found that a dram in the distillery manager's office, broken down with their own water on the spot, tastes better than the identical whisky broken down before maturing and bottling. I don't quite understand why this should be so. But it must be remembered that the local water is the most important single factor in determining the special characteristics of an individual Highland malt whisky. It is more important even than the peat, as is indicated by the fact that some great Highland malt distilleries get their ready peated malt from outside the region. (But even if you get the water right you can't necessarily make good whisky. Once in Australia they discovered a stream whose water was chemically identical with that which is used at Glenlivet distillery. They proceeded to make malt whisky, using that water and imported Scottish peat. When it was quite new, just off the still, it might have been the real thing. But on maturing it was terrible. This suggests that the climate is important in the maturing process. Temperature and humidity certainly affect the rate and quality of maturing.)

How much water should one add to one's whisky? This is very much a question of personal taste. I have known some real experts who drink single malt whisky with the same amount of water added, which seems a lot. Of course, much depends on the strength of the whisky and on when you are drinking it. With a normal 70° whisky I myself would add just a little Malvern water if drinking it before dinner and none at all if drinking it after dinner. A really well-matured Highland malt whisky of high proof – say a fifteen-year-old 100° Macallan, a bottle of which happens to catch my eye as I write – really needs the addition of some water, which serves to open out the flavour. I find that if I want to savour fully a whisky of this age, strength and quality, a few drops of water bring out its nose and 'release the natural oils'; one may want to add some more water after this initial tasting. The nose, incidentally, is the prime organ for determining the flavour of whisky. With a whisky of high proof, a good way is to rub some on the palms of both hands and then sniff your hands. I have done this with 119° malt whisky straight from the still, and it is amazing how precisely the flavours come through. First the flavour of the peat, and then, as the spirit evaporates on your hands, the flavour of the malt, with which you are left at the end. Professional tasters use this method and also use the 'nose glass', a tall tulip-shaped glass, rather like an outsize copita, in which the nose can be buried as the taster sniffs. The nose of a professional is a remarkably sensitive organ, though often its possessor may not be able to put into words exactly what he is looking for. One expert blender was once asked, as he went about sniffing samples of malt whisky from different distilleries, exactly what he was looking for. 'The smell of pear drops,' he replied. This is not as absurd as it may sound. Although I have not sucked a pear drop since my childhood in Edinburgh, I recollect now that the smell and flavour of that particular sweet is reminiscent of the first aroma that comes off a fine Eastern malt when sniffed.

How old should a whisky be? It is difficult to give a precise answer. The rate of maturing is affected by the atmospheric conditions of the warehouse in which the cask is stored as well as by the size of the cask. But in general I do not think a malt whisky should be drunk at under five years old. Though even five years is young – too young according to some whisky experts – I must say that I have had several eminently drinkable whiskies at that age. Whisky loses both strength and volume as it matures (it tends to lose strength in a humid atmosphere, whereas in a dry atmosphere there is more loss of bulk through absorption into the wood of the cask), and the Excise people allow a loss by evaporation and absorption of 2 per cent per year. (The loss of whisky in the cask during the maturing process is known as 'ullage', which is the difference between 'original' gallonage, the amount originally put into the cask, and 'regauge' gallonage, the amount remaining at a later date.) It is thus an expensive business keeping whisky in the wood for a long time. But it pays off in terms of improved flavour and quality up to, say, fifteen years. It is impossible to determine the optimum age for whisky in general terms; so much depends on the individual case. In 1967 I drank, at Longmorn distillery, whisky from a cask that was filled in April 1899 and just broached. By all the rules it should have gone 'woody' – and indeed, it should have evaporated, because a loss of 2 per cent per annum over sixty-eight years should yield less than nothing. But in fact it was not woody at all : it had lost strength and body, but it was mellow and pleasant though (surprisingly perhaps) without the character of a much younger Longmorn. Some whiskies are at their best at twelve years old : the managing director at Glenlivet distillery told me that in his view the twelve-year-old Glenlivet bottled by the company is as good as it can get. There is no doubt that some whiskies keep on improving, up to fifteen, twenty, twenty-five years or even longer. But it is possible to make too much of a fuss about mere age. I would rather have a superior whisky eight years old than an inferior twelve years old. As a general rule, I would say that ten years is a good drinking age for a single malt whisky, but some will be excellent a year or two younger and others will improve noticeably if left longer in the cask. As for blends, it will be remembered that the age (if any) stated on the label is the age of the youngest whisky in the blend. A blend labelled 'eight years old' is liable to contain some malts considerably older. The age of the malt whiskies in a blend is, of course, of first importance in determining the quality of that blend. It must be realized that all the greatest pot-still malt whiskies go largely for blending, and some go entirely for blending; and since most blends contain more than 50 per cent patent-still grain whisky, the quality of the malt whisky must be high if the resulting body and flavour is to reflect the malt content. Though for drinking neat or with water I personally prefer a single malt whisky, I must stress that all the reputable blends contain a proportion of some of the finest well-matured malts.

Whisky is a drink that can be taken before, with or after a meal. An Eastern malt with a little water before a meal, a good blend with quite a lot of water or soda with a meal, and a full, fruity malt drunk neat (as one would drink brandy) after a meal – this, to my taste, is the best way of taking it. Some foods, however, demand neat whisky. Haggis, for example, should be consumed with neat whisky, and in fact a blended Scotch whisky goes quite well with it. With fresh Scotch salmon, whisky (to my taste, a single malt) with quite a lot of water goes very well. But, of course, I would not insist on whisky with everything. A variety of dry white wines go admirably with salmon, and I am certainly not going to recommend that one should replace wine as a dinner drink with whisky. Each has its part to play in a well-ordered meal. But I do want to stress the versatility of Scotch whisky and its suitability for a great variety of occasions.

Here again one must consult one's own taste and the important thing is to give one's own taste a chance by experimenting freely and really paying attention as one drinks. Whisky is not a drink to be swilled. I need hardly say that, like all spirits, it must be drunk in moderation. Whisky to be savoured must be drunk in small quantities : the palate soon loses its power of discriminating and relishing if too much is drunk at once. I confess that in tasting whiskies in order to make up my mind about their quality I cannot go on for long without my palate becoming dulled (even if I do not swallow but spit out after tasting). Professional tasters have told me that the best time to taste whisky is in the morning before breakfast, before the palate has lost its edge after food has been taken or after smoking. One old stillman claims that at six o'clock every morning he takes a tumbler of neat whisky to 'clean out the tubes', but this is not a practice I would recommend. For the lay-man whisky is certainly not a pre-breakfast drink. I myself do not normally drink whisky before evening, though I have some glowing recollections of memorable exceptions to this rule. The knowing whisky drinker will surely appreciate lots of other drinks besides whisky. I do not normally drink before lunch on a working day, but if I do a dry sherry in winter and a campari and soda in summer is very likely to be my choice. On a damp, chilly day in Scotland, on the other hand, whisky is the right drink at almost any hour. And there can be special social occasions at any time when whisky is appropriate. Otherwise, 6 pm seems to be the earliest time when one's thoughts might well turn to a pre-prandial whisky. A malt whisky with a little Malvern water seems to me the best before-dinner drink in the world, and another drunk straight in a tall tulip-shaped wine glass (which enables you to savour the 'nose') at room temperature is a perfect after-dinner drink.

Blended Scotch whisky with ginger ale is now a very common drink, and so (in Scotland, surprisingly) is whisky and lemonade. I suspect that many people who drink these mixtures do so in order to give an alcoholic kick to their ginger ale or lemonade, in which case it seems rather a pity to use Scotch whisky at all. But there must also be many people who genuinely like the taste of the combination of Scotch and ginger ale or Scotch and lemonade. If they do, then more power to them. So long as they are not just drowning their Scotch whisky with some other flavour because they do not really like the taste of Scotch but feel that they ought to drink it for social reasons, and so long as they are not just adding alcohol for the kick, then nobody can object to their preferring the combination of flavours that pleases them. This goes for whisky cocktails too. Though conservative in my own whisky tastes, I am no purist in these matters. Just as I remain sceptical about all the mumbo-jumbo that goes with the drinking of wine and maintain that a man has a perfect right to drink any wine with any food if he is really tasting what he is drinking and genuinely likes it that way, so my only plea to Scotch whisky drinkers is that they attend to what they drink and base their preference on a decision deliberately made from a number of alternatives on the basis of genuine gustatory enjoyment.

Taste is notoriously difficult to describe, and the taste of a good Scotch whisky is so subtly compounded of bouquet, the actual taste on the palate, the after-taste, and the pleasing intellectual and physical glow that accompanies its consumption, that one man's account of his experience in drinking a given whisky may be very different from that of another who enjoys it equally. If, therefore, I now proceed to give some account of my experience of different pot-still malt whiskies, it is on the understanding that the reader will bear these reservations in mind. About blended whiskies I will add nothing to the scattered remarks I have made throughout this book, except to say once again that the drinker should select his brand thoughtfully and not drink merely out of habit or convention. And let him test the claims of advertisers on his own palate.

Let me make it clear at the outset that I do not believe it possible to arrange Highland malt whiskies in a simple order of merit. This is not only because an individual whisky will vary from year to year – not so much as a wine from a single vineyard will, but still perceptibly – and according to its age. There is also the question of individual taste and the time, mood and circumstances in which the whisky is drunk. There are times when I have felt like a full, peaty Islay whisky and other times when I have preferred a more delicate and fragrant Eastern malt. I have found, too – and I am sure that my experience cannot be unique here – that my actual palate is not constant: when I first tasted Clynelish, for example, it seemed to me a rich, full, robust yet gentle whisky with a mellow fruity quality quite different from the characteristic 'medicinal' fullness of, say, Laphroaig. Yet later, tasting the identical Clynelish, I could perceive a definite relationship with the Laphroaig kind of peatiness. As for Laphroaig itself, perhaps the most distinctive of all Scotch whiskies, sometimes I feel that its special quality (which I have heard described by a novice on his first drinking it as suggestive of iodine) is exactly what I am in the mood for – a whisky idiosyncratic enough to stand up to other strong flavours that one may have been tasting, admirable for rounding off a meal which has included highly seasoned food. At other times again I prefer my Laphroaig in the blend 'Islay Mist', which retains the fullness of Laphroaig but with only a touch of its strong 'medicinal' flavour, very soft and mellow. (I myself would not use the term 'medicinal' to describe the flavour of Laphroaig, but I know what people mean when they use it and I cannot think of a really descriptive term that fits. Some say they can taste seaweed, and it may well be that the characteristic Islay peat does contain sea vegetation, which explains this.) 'Islay Mist' contains Laphroaig, Smith's Glenlivet and Glen Grant, blended together with grain whisky. It is one of the very best blends.

The Laphroaig I have enjoyed as an after-dinner drink in the suitable conditions described is ten years old and 75° proof, bottled by the distillery; the 'Islay Mist' is eight years old and 70° proof. (Perhaps I ought to remind American readers once again that British proof is calculated differently from American and that I am using British proof percentages: British 70° proof is American 80° proof.) The Clynelish which sometimes seems to me to bear a similarity in its kind of fullness and body to Laphroaig but at other times seems softer and less pungent, is twelve years old, 70° proof, bottled by Ainslie and Heilbron. I always find it, whatever the state of my palate, a splendid whisky, especially when drunk neat after dinner. I have tried George Saintsbury's recipe of mixing half Clynelish with half Glenlivet, and the result is a very fine drink indeed.

If I feel like an Islay whisky but do not want its Islay features to be quite so pronounced as they are in Laphroaig, I drink Lagavulin bottled by White Horse Distillers at 75° proof (no age is given on the label). This is an admirable robust whisky with just enough of the Islay kind of peatiness to give it distinctive character. I have drunk an even better Lagavulin at the distillery on a wet and windy day when one realized how appropriate to the climate of the island Islay whisky is.[38] Of the other Islay whiskies, I have tasted Bowmore at the distillery and more recently bought a bottle at the duty-free shop at Heathrow; quite some time ago I bought a bottle of Ardbeg at a licensed grocer's in Crieff, bottled by D. & J. MacEwen of Stirling. Each has its own version of the Islay taste. Of the other island whiskies, Talisker, the Skye whisky, is the best known. This is available at a number of ages and strengths: the best I have tasted is the 100° proof bottled by Gordon & Macphail (no age on the label). If you breathe the flavour out of your nose immediately after swallowing, you get an after-taste of a kind of oily smokiness which I find extremely agreeable. Talisker is not perhaps to everybody's taste, nor is it an all-purpose whisky; but it is a whisky of great character, and certainly the whisky to be drunk in Skye itself when a light rain is falling and the mist is on the hills. And, of course, one does not need to go to Skye for this appropriate situation to present itself.

Across the water from Islay are the two Campbeltown distilleries, Springbank and Glen Scotia. In Springbank distillery the foreshots and the feints are re-distilled in a second, separate still (instead of being run back through the feints receiver to be re-distilled with the next batch of low wines in the low wines still). This may account for Springbank's special kind of mellowness and lightness. It is a rich yet not at all a heavy whisky, soft, fragrant, not peaty, and quite unlike the traditional heavily peated and very full-bodied Campbeltown. I have recently drunk an 80° Springbank, bottled by Eaglesome Ltd. 'over twelve years old'; it is a beautifully smooth and gentle whisky that has perhaps more finish than individuality. Very different is Glen Scotia, full bodied and heavily peated, with a rich 'nose' and a fine robustness of flavour. A. Gillies & Co. (the owners) bottle an eight-year-old at 75° proof.

It was an accident of illustration that made me start this tasting tour with Islay whiskies. The more obvious thing to do would be to begin with Glenlivet and then work north and west. But since I have been talking of the whiskies of Islay and Skye, perhaps I had better stay with the islands before moving back to the mainland and go on now to Orkney, where Highland Park is an outstanding whisky. (I have never tasted Scapa, the other Orkney whisky, as a single whisky, nor have I spoken to anyone who has.) Highland Park is regularly bottled at 75°. It is a rich, heavy whisky with a peaty nose. The 100° proof bottled by Gordon & Macphail is even better: the full yet subtle flavour seduces the nose as soon as it approaches the glass. The 100° proof reduced with water just after being poured from the bottle tastes more full-flavoured than the 75° proof reduced with water to the same strength, just as the 100° proof poured from the bottle and reduced with water to 75° proof tastes better than that bottled at 75° and drunk neat. This is a phenomenon I have noted before. It does not apply to all whiskies, but it does so noticeably to Highland Park.

Let us now cross the Pentland Firth and come to the mainland of Scotland. The most northerly distillery on the mainland is Pulteney, which produces 'Old Pulteney'. This is a whisky I have known about ever since I read Neil Gunn's book on whisky in 1935, but it was only in 1967 that

I was able to get some (bottled at 85° proof, eight years old). It has a splendid fruitiness (as distinct from a peatiness), the tasted flavour fulfilling most interestingly and complexly the promise of its 'nose'. For some time I have been preaching it with all the enthusiasm of a convert, and I hope that the distillers, or Hiram Walker who are now the parent company, will make more of it available as a single whisky. Coming down the Caithness coast into Sutherland, one comes to Clynelish distillery. Let me once again raise my hat to Clynelish, that fine, full, mellow whisky, before moving down into Ross and Cromarty and the distilleries of Balblair, Glenmorangie and Dalmore. Balblair is a pleasing light-bodied whisky of distinctive flavour. Glenmorangie, only a few miles away, is very different: it has a special kind of floweriness, a delicate yet unmistakable fragrance, that I find extremely attractive. It is bottled at 70°, ten years old, and is steadily becoming more available in England. Glenmorangie is what I would call an all-purpose whisky. It is equally good as a pre-prandial and as a post-prandial drink, and I confess I have drunk it at many other times as well. There is a Glenmorangie which I have drunk at the distillery which is older and more full-bodied than that which is available bottled, possessing more richness and less delicacy than the latter. It goes for blending, of course, but anyone lucky enough to get a dram of it at the distillery will have a memorable experience. Dalmore is a heavier whisky altogether, peatier, full-bodied and – one doesn't want to over-use this word, but it is inevitable here – robust. I have some bottled at 70° proof by Duncan Macbeth & Co. of Invergordon. William Cadenhead of Aberdeen bottles both a twelve-year-old and a twenty-year-old at 75° proof. It is an excellent after-dinner drink.

Continuing south from Ross-shire to Inverness-shire we come to Glen Mhor distillery at Inverness. Glen Mhor is one of the truly great post-prandial whiskies, full, rich and mellow, slightly less peaty than Dalmore and with a smoother finish. The ten-year-old bottled by Charles Mackinlay & Co. of Leith at 75° proof shows its paces admirably. Glen Mhor is a 'bigger' whisky than a characteristic Speyside whisky, but it has some of the qualities of a Glenlivet.

Going north-east from Inverness to Elgin and then south from Elgin we approach the great heartland of Highland malt whisky. I can only pick out some of the many fine malt whiskies produced in this region and discuss those I know best. On the south side of Elgin is Linkwood, a fairly light-bodied whisky with a 'nose' not (it seems to me) unlike Glenlivet, though less full. It has a pleasing light fragrance : I would class it as an all-purpose whisky. Some miles south of Elgin there is Longmorn, the distillery where I once drank a sixty-eight-year-old whisky from a newly broached cask. Longmorn is a full, virile whisky with a fine 'nose', admirable when drunk neat after dinner but also most agreeable with a little water pre-prandially or indeed at any time. It is bottled at 70° proof by William Cadenhead of Aberdeen.

Continuing down to the road from Elgin to Craigellachie (and ignoring perforce some excellent distilleries) we come to Glen Rothes-Glenlivet distillery, whose whisky is bottled at 80° proof, ten years old, by William Cadenhead. Glen Rothes has a strong, peaty 'nose'; if not the subtlest it is one of the fullest of the Eastern malts, a whisky of real character. Then on through Craigellachie to the great cluster of Speyside distilleries. Glenlivet I have already discussed at length, but I will add just a word about its distinctive qualities to the palate. At its best, Smith's Glenlivet combines a teasing subtlety of flavour with a distinctive 'nose' and fullness. These are not always sufficiently in evidence when it is bottled too young, but the firm's own bottling, twelve years old at 80°, gives one everything that could be desired in this noble whisky. I have tasted a Glenlivet put in cask in 1941 and bottled (by Berry Brothers & Rudd) in 1958, and the only note on it which I entered in my whisky scrap-book after the first glass was simply 'a superb whisky'. But later experience of comparing different ages and proofs leads me to believe that additional age over twelve years does not add all that much in quality, and (within limits of course) a twelve-year-old at a higher proof tastes better than an older whisky at a lower proof. But the twelve-year-old is decidedly better than anything younger. I have on my desk as I write an eight-year-old Glenlivet at 70° and the distillery's twelve-year-old at 80° proof. The eight-year-old is a good whisky, it is true, but its 'nose' is less subtle (in the twelve-year-old the sweetness mingles with the peatiness and the fullness in a most intriguing way, while in the younger whisky the flavours seems less integrated) and it is less smooth and less rounded in flavour. All the same, if an eight-year-old Smith's Glenlivet is all you can get, then seize it : it is a very good dram.

How does Glenlivet compare with Glen Grant? In general character they are not dissimilar : each has that smooth integration of peatiness, softness and full sweetness (or almost sweetness) that needs age to bring out. Like Glenlivet, Glen Grant is conspicuously better at ten or, better still, twelve years old than at, say, five (and it is available at five years old). There is a sharpness about a young Glen Grant that belies its true potential. I once compared a seventeen-year-old Glen Grant with a ten-year-old, and I noted in my whisky scrap-book that it was not the first sip of each that showed the real difference, 'but after steady comparative sipping the superior mellowness of the seventeen-year-old as against the ten-year-old became evident'. A well-matured Glen Grant has a splendid smoothness : it is not, perhaps, such a complexly patterned whisky in the combination of 'nose', taste and after-taste that is found in Glenlivet at its best, being a more single-minded whisky, as it were. At one time I used to drink a twelve-year-old Glen Grant matured in plain oak as my favourite whisky. But I have grown to like the finish given by maturing in sherry wood, and I have also outgrown any belief that I have a single favourite malt whisky. I pay my respects equally to those two whisky classics, Glenlivet and Glen Grant. The latter, by the way, is readily available in a variety of bottlings.

Moving north-west of Glenlivet to Dufftown, we come to Mortlach distillery, one of the many clustered in that area.

I have a special fondness for Mortlach, because it was the all-purpose whisky I drank regularly during the five years I lived in Ithaca, N.Y., and taught at Cornell University. I used to get it sent up from Macy's in New York. It is a fine, full Eastern malt, with a rich but not a specially peaty flavour. Glenfiddich and Dufftown, two nearby distilleries, produce excellent whiskies too; the former has a pleasing dry fragrance and the latter is the more peaty. Macallan distillery in nearby Craigellachie produces a Speyside whisky of great individuality. The 100° proof bottled by Gordon & Macphail has a powerful 'nose' which proclaims very accurately the flavour to the palate, which I find difficult to describe as its special kind of richness is neither peaty nor flowery but something in between. On the other side of the Spey from Macallan distillery is Aberlour-Glenlivet founded in 1879 and controlled by the Campbell Group of Companies in Glasgow. Campbells bottle an eight-year-old 100° proof Aberlour-Glenlivet, a fragrant malt of real individuality : it is now fairly readily available in England (and at the duty-free shop at Heathrow). In Keith (the third in the triangle of whisky towns of which the other two are Dufftown and Craigellachie) Strathisla distillery produces a whisky with a full, fragrant flavour which seems to come somewhere between Glenlivet and Mortlach. Further to the south-west, near Ballindalloch on the Spey, Glenfarclas distillery produces a somewhat peatier whisky, full-bodied and assertive. (This was another whisky I used to drink in Ithaca, New York : it was the only Highland malt sold by the local liquor store I dealt with, and very satisfying it was.)

Once again I must point out that I am picking out some of the whiskies that I know best; those I have discussed do not represent all the good single malt whiskies. But I must add, before I conclude this somewhat impressionistic survey, three Lowland malts that I know. One is Rosebank, now available as a single whisky bottled at 70° proof, a pleasant, smooth whisky, sharper to the nose than to the palate, the second is Glenkinchie, which so far as I know is not available as a single whisky but of which I have a sample bottle from an Edinburgh blending firm. This too is a very agreeable whisky, slightly sweeter and perhaps just a trifle sharper than Rosebank. The third is Auchentoshan, a well-rounded if not very individual whisky. I should like to beat the drum a bit for Lowland malts. They have been overshadowed in the literature on whisky and in the esteem of single whisky drinkers by Highland malts, which have more romance in their story and the best of which, it is true, are whiskies of greater character and grander flavour. But a well-matured Lowland malt is – especially for those who do not prefer a heavily peated whisky – a pleasant and civilized drink of distinctive quality and makes a good all-purpose whisky.

Scotch whisky is one of Scotland's great contributions to the good life. Like any alcoholic drink, it is capable of abuse, but the best guarantee against abuse is knowledge and discrimination. As we look back on its long story, remembering the farmer-distillers of the seventeenth and eighteenth centuries, the proud smugglers of the days when the Government was desperately fumbling for ways of taxing and controlling whisky production, the invention of the Coffey still and its momentous consequences, the flamboyant *entrepreneurs* of the latter part of the nineteenth century, and the world-wide reputation of Scotch whisky today, we cannot but marvel at the way in which a spontaneous Highland activity which fitted in so well with the rhythms of the agricultural year has become over the years a vast industry. And I have my more personal memories : celebrating a wedding anniversary with fresh-caught salmon and a bottle of Glen Grant in the kitchen of a little house by the Moray Firth; landing up in a little Banffshire pub after a wet day's trout-fishing to warm myself with the spirit distilled all around me; talking with fellow writers and poets on a summer evening in a Rose Street pub in Edinburgh with drams of a variety of Highland malts standing on the bar between us; sipping Clynelish after dinner at home with a few academic friends as we planned the development of the University of Sussex; arriving at the house of a friend in New Jersey to find that he had ordered in some Mortlach because he knew I was coming and had heard that I liked that particular whisky; celebrating Hogmanay sitting on a bed in a hotel room in Agra with two friends and a bottle of Glenlivet after visiting the Taj Mahal by moonlight; drinking a nameless but obviously authentic blended Scotch from a lemonade bottle full of the liquor supplied by a friendly clerk at Belgrade airport as I waited a weary time for the airport to be cleared of the top brass and security officers awaiting the arrival of President Tito; drinking with courteous distillery managers at distilleries all over Scotland; and innumerable occasions, domestic, convivial, celebratory or merely casual, gratifying the palate and warming the spirit with this great drink. The proper drinking of Scotch whisky is more than indulgence : it is a toast to civilization, a tribute to the continuity of culture, a manifesto of man's determination to use the resources of nature to refresh mind and body and enjoy to the full the senses with which he has been endowed. And so I conclude with Robert Burns's great hail to the barley from which Scotch whisky derives :

> Let husky wheat the haughs adorn   *meadows*
> An' aits set up their awnie horn,   *bearded*
> An' pease and beans, an e'en or morn,
>   Perfume the plain :
> Leeze me on thee, John Barleycorn   *blessings on*
>   Thou king o' grain !

To which we may add :
> Freedom an' whisky gang thegither,
>   Tak aff your dram !

Appendix

THE DISTILLERIES OF SCOTCH WHISKY

1 Aberfeldy
2 Aberlour-Glenlivet
3 Allt A Bhainne
4 Ardbeg
5 Ardmore
6 Auchentoshan
7 Auchriosk
8 Aultmore Glenlivet
9 Braes of Glenlivet
10 Balblair
11 Balmenach-Glenlivet
12 Balvenie-Glenlivet
13 Banff
14 BenNevis
14 *Ben Nevis*
15 Benriach
16 Benrinnes
17 Benromach-Glenlivet
18 Ben Wyvis
19 Bladnoch
20 Blair Atholl
21 Bowmore
22 Bruichladdich
23 Bunnahabhain
24 *Caledonian*
25 *Cambus*
26 *Cameronbridge*
27 Caol Ila
28 Caperdonich
29 Cardow
30 *Carsebridge*
31 Clynelish

32 Coleburn-Glenlivet
33 Convalmore-Glenlivet
34 Cragganmore-Glenlivet
35 Craigellachie-Glenlivet
36 Dailuaine-Glenlivet
37 Dallas Dhu
38 Dalmore
39 Dalwhinnie
40 Deanston
41 Dufftown-Glenlivet
42 *Dumbarton*
43 Edradour
44 Fettercairn
45 *Girvan*
46 Glen Albyn
47 Glenallachie-Glenlivet
48 Glenburgie-Glenlivet
49 Glencadam
50 Glendronach
51 Glendullan-Glenlivet
52 Glen Elgin-Glenlivet
53 Glenfarclas-Glenlivet
54 Glenfiddich
55 Glenfyne
56 Glengarioch
57 Glenglassaugh
58 Glengoyne
59 Glen Grant-Glenlivet
60 Glen Keith-Glenlivet
61 Glenkinchie
62 Glenlivet, The
63 Glenlochy

64 Glenlossie
65 Glen Mhor
66 Glenmorangie
67 Glen Moray-Glenlivet
68 Glen Rothes-Glenlivet
69 Glen Scotia
70 Glen Spey
71 Glentauchers
72 Glenturret
73 Glenugie
74 Glenury-Royal
75 Highland Park
76 Hillside
77 Imperial-Glenlivet
78 Inchgower
79 *Invergordon*
80 Inverleven
81 Jura
82 Kinclaith
83 Knockando
84 Knockdhu
85 Ladyburn
86 Lagavulin
87 Laphroaig
88 Ledaig
89 Linkwood-Glenlivet
90 Littlemill
91 Loch Lomond
92 Lochnagar Royal
93 Lochside
93 *Lochside*
94 Lomond
95 Longmorn-Glenlivet
96 Macallan-Glenlivet

97 Macduff
98 Millburn
99 Miltonduff-Glenlivet
100 Moffat
100 *Moffat*
101 Mortlach
102 *North British*
103 North Port
104 *North of Scotland*
105 Oban
106 Ord
107 Pittyvaich
108 *Port Dundas*
109 Port Ellen
110 Pulteney
111 Rosebank
112 Royal Brackla
113 St Magdalene
114 Scapa
115 Speyburn-Glenlivet
116 Speyside
117 Springbank
118 *Strathclyde*
119 Strathisla-Glenlivet
120 Strathmill
121 *Strathmore*
122 Talisker
123 Tamdhu-Glenlivet
124 Tamnavulin
125 Teaninich
126 Tomatin
127 Tomintoul-Glenlivet
128 Tormore
129 Tullibardine

Italic Names=Grain Distilleries
Bold Numbers=Names inset on map

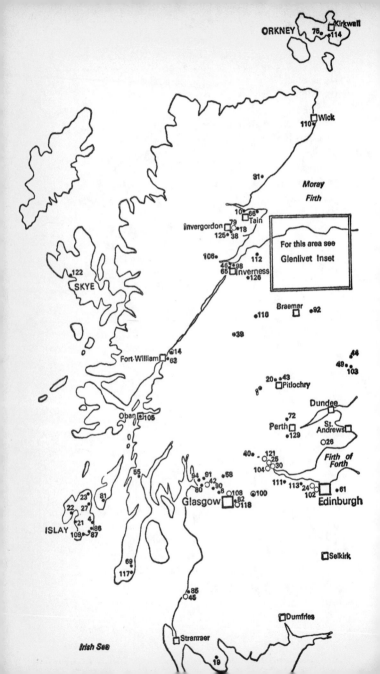

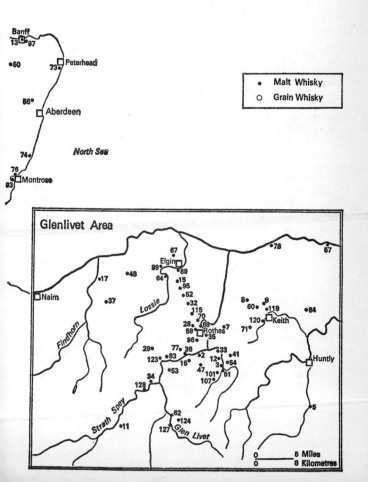

The Distilleries of Scotch Whisky

Banff
13 97
• 50
73 • Peterhead
58 •
Aberdeen
74 • North Sea
76 •
93 Montrose

Legend:
- • Malt Whisky
- ○ Grain Whisky

Glenlivet Area

67
Elgin
99 89
• 17 • 48 64 • 15
Nairn 95
• 37 • 52
• 32
J 15
70
28 • 68
59 Rothes • 7
96 • 35
29 • 77 • 36 • 33
123 • 83 16 • 2 • 41
• 53 47 12 • 54
101 • 3
107 51
34
128
62
• 11 124
127 Glen Livet

• 78 57
8 • 9
60 • • 119
• 84
120 Keith
71 •
Huntly
• 5

Findhorn
Lossie
Strath Spey

0   5 Miles
0   8 Kilometres

Notes

1   A word about 'Scotch' and 'Scottish'. In Scotland the adjective 'Scotch' is frowned on and 'Scottish' or 'Scots' preferred. But 'Scotch' is allowed for whisky. As a schoolboy in Edinburgh I was taught that 'Scotch' could only be used for Scotch whisky and Scotch broth.

2   It is the home-grown barley especially, which contains about 20 per cent of moisture, that requires this special drying to reduce its moisture content to about 10 per cent or a little over: some imported barley is lighter and drier than the domestic barley and thus is less in need of drying.

3   This should be 40 to 45 per cent after soaking.

4   In the course of germination the barley-seed develops two enzymes (an enzyme is an organic substance produced by living cells which acts as a catalyst), the enzyme cystase, which breaks down the cellulose enclosing the insoluble starch cells and so makes the starch accessible for growth, and the enzyme diastase, which converts the insoluble starch which the action of the cystase has made available into dextrin, a soluble form of starch. The diastase also changes the dextrin into maltose, a readily soluble sugar. It is the sugar which eventually produces alcohol.

5   The enzymes are maltase and zymase: maltase acts on the maltose to produce dextrose (otherwise glucose, colourless crystalline soluble sugar), and zymase converts the dextrose into alcohol and carbon dioxide. Dextrose is $C_6H_{12}O_6$ and alcohol is C_2H_5OH: what happens is represented by the equation: $C_6H_{12}O_6 — 2C_2H_5OH + 2CO_2$.

6   It is with the stage of fermenting that the excise officer becomes interested, for according to the fall in density between the wort and the wash he will be able to work out the amount of spirit to be expected in the end. This is because the density of the wort decreases as the dextrose is converted into alcohol. There will thus be a decrease in the specific gravity of the liquid from something like 1·05 (the specific gravity of the original wort) to say 0·998, the specific gravity of the wash. A decrease from a specific gravity of 1·05 to one of 0·998 represents an attenuation of 52 degrees. Every

degree of attenuation in 10,000 gallons represents—or should represent—at the end of the day more than twenty gallons of proof spirit. So the excise officer should know how much whisky to look for once the fermentation process is over.

7   It has recently been announced that, with the decimalization of the British coinage and weights and measures, a new standard of British proof will be worked out.

8   Scotch whisky is defined in the Finance Acts 1969 as: 'Spirits which have been distilled from a mash of cereals which has been—

  i saccharified by the diastase of malt contained therein with or without natural diastases approved for the purpose by the Commissioners of Customs & Excise; and

  ii fermented by the action of yeast; and

  iii distilled at less than 166·4 degrees proof in such a way that the distillate has an aroma and flavour derived from the materials used, and which have been matured in wooden casks for a period of at least three years.'

The Act also provides that 'the expression "Scotch whisky" shall mean whisky which has been distilled in Scotland'.

9   The terminology is not consistently employed. Campbeltowns and Islays may also be regarded as Highland Malts, from which the Highland Malts produced in the north-east of Scotland are often distinguished by being called Eastern Malts.

10   Rye was used, with barley, in the Canonmills distillery of John Haig in the 1780s. See below, p. 89.

11   *Baul* in 'usquebaugh-baul' is the Gaelic word *ball*, meaning member, part of the body.

12   'We supped well; and after supper, Mr Johnson, whom I had not seen taste any fermented liquor during all our expedition, had a gill of whisky brought to him. "Come," said he, "let me know what it is that makes a Scotsman happy." He drank it all but a drop, which I begged leave to pour into my glass, that I might say we had drunk whisky together.' *Boswell's Journal of a Tour to the Hebrides with Samuel Johnson*, ed. Pottle and Bennett, London, 1936, p. 348.

13   Whisky and milk was the breakfast drink of the American poet John Malcolm Brinnin when he entertained Dylan Thomas on his last, fatal visit to the United States.

14   The Gin Act of 1736, aimed at the peculiarly English problem of excessive gin drinking, exempted Scotland, and henceforward (until 1855) the duties on spirits distilled in England and Scotland differed. English distillers objected to the lower Scottish duty, so that an Act of 1751 imposed an equalizing duty on Scottish spirit exported to England.

15   Scotch whisky imported into England in the eighteenth and

first half of the nineteenth century was more often than not 'rectified' (re-distilled and flavoured) and turned into gin.

16   Soda water, or aerated water, is water charged with carbon dioxide and was first artificially produced in England in the eighteenth century, when it was regarded as beneficial to health. Large-scale commercial manufacture was begun at Geneva in 1790 by Nicholas Paul, and it was Paul's partner, J. Schweppe, who started its commercial manufacture in London and founded the firm which still flourishes. Sodium bicarbonate was sometimes added to the water before carbonation, and originally the term 'soda water' referred only to carbonated water which also contained sodium bicarbonate. But soon it came to describe carbonated water both with and without sodium bicarbonate. (In the United States the term was extended to apply to any sparkling drink—hence 'soda fountain'.) Various other salts were sometimes added to carbonated water, to produce potash water, lithia water, etc. When I was a boy the standard soda water produced by the Scottish mineral-water firm of Dunbar and seen regularly on the sideboards of Edinburgh families was labelled 'potash water'.

The soda water siphon, standard in Britain but not in the United States where the individual small sealed bottle is preferred, was developed from the 'Regency portable fountain' patented by Charles Plinth in 1825. In 1837 Antoine Perpigna patented his 'vase siphoïde', which substituted for the stopcock of the Regency portable fountain a valve closed by a spring. A tube reached from the bottom of the siphon to the curved spout, and the pressure of the gas forced the soda water out when the valve was opened. This is essentially the modern siphon

17   The pamphlet was produced in an effort to influence opinion against a 'Sale of Whisky Bill' introduced into the Commons by Sir Herbert Maxwell. The Bill would have prevented patent-still whisky from being sold as whisky. It did not survive its first reading.

18   This odd point about sedentary drinkers crops up again and again in the arguments of the grain distillers and the blenders. The Scotch Whisky Association's pamphlet *Scotch Whisky: Questions & Answers* (Edinburgh, 1967) repeats the ritual statement that 'pot-still whisky is too strongly flavoured for most people in sedentary occupations'.

19   It has been suggested to me by a well-known figure in the Scotch whisky trade that 'Vat 69' sells well on the Continent because it is regarded as a sex symbol. Dewars continues to be the best selling of DCL whiskies in America. 'J. & B. Rare' and 'Cutty Sark' (both whiskies with a high proportion of patent-still grain whisky and certainly not to my own taste) are the over-all best

owned by J. & G. Grant Ltd.; Tomatin is owned by Tomatin Distillers Ltd., a public company; Longmorn-Glenlivet and nearby Benriach are owned by The Glenlivet Distilleries Ltd. The attractive little distillery of Edradour near Pitlochry is owned by the firm of William Whitley & Co. of Leith (a nineteenth-century firm which has since 1922 been a subsidiary of Glenforres Distillery Company, a large and active company which produces a great variety of blends, including 'House of Lords' and 'King's Ransom'). Of the two Campbeltown distilleries Glen Scotia was owned by A. Gillies & Co. (Distillers) Ltd. from 1955 to 1970, when the firm was absorbed in Amalgamated Distilled Products Ltd., and Springbank, which was built by the Mitchell family in 1823, is owned by J. & A. Mitchell & Co. Ltd. The Islay distillery of Bruichladdich, attractively situated on the shores of Loch Indaal, is owned by Invergordon Distilleries Ltd. Bowmore distillery, opposite Bruichladdich on the other side of the loch, is own by Sherriff's Bowmore Distillery Ltd., whose principal Director is S. P. Morrison of Stanley P. Morrison Ltd., Glasgow whisky brokers. Ardbeg distillery, a little up the east coast of Islay from Lagavulin, Laphroaig and Port Ellen, is independently owned. The Islay distilleries are all picturesquely situated on the seashore.

I do not know how many blends of Scotch whisky there are now on the market but I do know that I am continuously being surprised at discovering new blends I had never heard of before. Now long ago the manager of a very large liquor store in the United States showed me his 'bin book', and the number of different blended Scotches listed there astonished me. The quality of course varies greatly. One is liable to find more inferior blends abroad than at home, because blenders abroad can do what they like with whiskies of different ages and qualities imported in cask. Unscrupulous traders can also re-fill labelled bottles with whisky not of the quality described on the label. In some South American countries whisky must be sold in bottles which have special tops which allow the contents to be poured out but do not allow anything to be poured in: I have seen such tops on bottles being filled for the South American market at Dewar's bottling plant at Inveralmond. There does not appear to be any significant variation in quality – that is, in the proportion of well-matured fine Highland malts in the blend – among the great number of standard blended Scotches put out by firms in DCL, though there are clearly discernible differences in body, sweetness, peatiness, sharpness to the nose, and other aspects of taste and smell. Many of these differences are not, however, discernible to the casual drinker and only become apparent if one has learned to know a particular blend very well (drinking it neat or with water) and then tries a different one. A trained taster can, of course, tell differences at once, and by smell only. But I repeat a point I have made before : most drinkers of whisky and soda (and *a fortiori* of whisky and ginger ale or whisky with any highly flavoured mixer) who ask for a particular brand would not know the difference if given a brand other than the one they ordered if it came out of a bottle which bore the label of the brand demanded. It is not unknown for a barman to say, on being asked for a particular blend, 'We've run out of it here; I'll just bring some from the other bar,' and return with a glass allegedly of the requested blend but actually of some other one. In the great majority of cases he gets away with it. Nor is it unknown – I am speaking of experiences in Britain which I can vouch for – for barmen simply to serve a different whisky from the one demanded on the (generally justified) assumption that the drinker will not taste the difference. In such a case he has his back to the customer when pouring the whisky and arranges that the customer does not see what bottle it comes from.

But in fact most Scotch whisky drinkers, in Britain at least, do not ask for a blend by name, but simply ask for a 'whisky' or a 'Scotch'. The blenders, who after all spend a great deal of effort in getting their blend right, resent this, and I think it is true to say that most of them would prefer to have customers ask for a specific blend even if it is not their own : it is the habit of specifying the blend that they want to encourage.[29] The increasing take-over of pubs and hotels in England by breweries has led to a restriction in the number of blends available, for the brewers understandably prefer to push the blends of the firms with which they have a business connection. The ramifications are often complicated. 'Queen Anne', a blend previously produced by Hill Thomson but now produced by The Glenlivet Distilleries Ltd. which absorbed Hill Thomson in 1972, is now sold in the 6000 pubs owned by the brewing firm of Courage, because Courage is a subsidiary of Imperial Group (best known for its cigarettes and tobaccos) which has acquired $27\frac{1}{2}\%$ of the shares in Glenlivet Distilleries. (10% of the shares in Glenlivet Distilleries are owned by the largest Japanese distillery group, Suntory). In 1970 the brewery firm of Bass Charrington took over the UK marketing of 'Vat 69', so that blend became the 'pouring whisky' of Bass Charrington's 10,000 pubs.

In an earlier chapter I discussed the 'Big Five' of DCL – Haig, Dewar, Walker, Buchanan, Mackie (White Horse) – and a sixth who really belongs with them, Sanderson. But, of course, there are many admirable smaller firms in DCL, some of them long established. D. & J. McCallum Ltd. of Edinburgh, for example, goes back to 1807 when the brothers Duncan and John McCallum established themselves as wine and spirit merchants and innkeepers. Their inn, popularly known as the 'Tattie Pit', was a well-known Edinburgh rendezvous. The brothers' wine and spirit business expanded, and on their death (they had both remained bachelors) it was taken over by their nephew Duncan Stewart, who developed McCallum's 'Perfection' blend. McCallums own Glenlochy distillery in Fort William. The firm merged with DCL in 1953. McCallum's head office is at 4 Picardy Place, at the east end of Edinburgh's 'New Town', a handsome Georgian house with fine Adam interior decoration and fireplaces. McCallum's 'Perfection' is one of the few whiskies to call itself on the label 'Scots whisky' rather than 'Scotch whisky'. It is exported to more than sixty countries, with especially important markets in Australia and New Zealand.

John Begg was one of the many Scotsmen who took

advantage of the 1823 Act to build a legitimate distillery. He built Lochnagar distillery, near Balmoral, in 1825, and Queen Victoria visited it, with Prince Albert, the Prince of Wales, Prince Alfred and the Princess Royal on 12 September 1848. John Begg recorded the event in his journal. He asked Prince Albert if he would like to taste a dram. 'HRH having agreed to this, I called for a bottle and glasses (which had been previously in readiness) and, presenting one glass to Her Majesty, she tasted it. So did His Royal Highness the Prince. I then presented a glass to the Princess Royal, and to the Prince of Wales, and Prince Alfred, all of whom tasted the spirit.' As a result of this visit, Lochnagar distillery was allowed to call itself 'Royal', which it does to this day. (The only previous granting of the appellation 'royal' to a distillery had been to Captain William Fraser of Brackla distillery by King William IV in 1835. As an advertisement in the *Morning Chronicle* put it at the time : 'His Majesty, having been pleased to distinguish this "by his royal Command to supply his Establishment", has placed this Whisky first on the list of British Spirits . . .' The Royal Brackla distillery is now owned by John Bisset.) A single malt from the Royal Lochnagar distillery is not, unfortunately, now available except to privileged visitors to the distillery. It almost all goes for blending – to Sanderson for 'Vat 69' as well as to 'John Begg' itself, a well-established blend and the only whisky I know of which once, in a Glasgow Jewish newspaper, advertised in Yiddish, translating its erstwhile advertising slogan 'Take a peg of John Begg' into 'Nem a schmeck fun Dzon Bek'. John Begg has been in DCL since 1916.

Other blending companies in DCL include Bulloch, Lade, which has owned the Islay distillery of Caol Ila since 1857 and merged with DCL in 1927 : its de luxe blend, 'Old Rarity', is highly esteemed by many who like a light-bodied whisky bottled at a slightly higher proof than is normal. Its regular blend is 'BL Gold Label'. There is also the Leith blending firm of A. & A. Crawford, dating from 1860, which joined DCL in 1944. They have two long-established blends, 'Three Star' and, a de luxe blend, 'Five Star', both a *local* product, and I should like to encourage discriminating Scotch whisky drinkers to take an interest in the localities from which their favourite whiskies come. Wine connoisseurs make pilgrimages to French vineyards. We are now beginning to see signs that some visitors to Scotland want to make a special whisky pilgrimage.

Select Bibliography

ALFRED BARNARD, *The Whisky Distilleries of the United Kingdom*. Newton Abbot, 1969. (Originally London, 1887.)

NEIL M. GUNN, *Whisky and Scotland*. London, 1935.

SIR ROBERT BRUCE LOCKHART, *Scotch: The Whisky of Scotland in Fact and Story*. London, 1951.

R. J. S. MCDOWALL, *The Whiskies of Scotland*. London, 1967.

J. M. ROBB, *Scotch Whisky: An Illustrated Guide*. London and Edinburgh, 1950.

S. W. SILLETT, *Illicit Scotch*. Aberdeen, 1965.

ROSS WILSON, *Scotch Made Easy*. London, 1959.
            Scotch, the Formative Years. London, 1970.

DCL and Scotch Whisky. The Distillers Company Ltd., London, 1973.

Scotch Whisky: Questions and Answers. The Scotch Whisky Association, Edinburgh, 1967.

Glenlivet, being the Annals of the Glenlivet Distillery. The Glenlivet Distillery, 1964.

JAMES LAVER, *The House of Haig*. Markinch, 1958.

ROSS WILSON, *The House of Sanderson*, 1963.

The North British Distillery Company Limited 1885–1960. Edinburgh. n.d.

R. J. FORBES, *Short History of the Art of Distilling*. Leiden, 1948.

GEORGE SAINTSBURY, *Notes on a Cellar-Book*. London, 1920.

CAPTAIN EDWARD BURT, *Letters from a Gentleman in the North of Scotland to his Friend in London*, 2 vols. London, 1754.

J. G. FYFE (ed.), *Scottish Diaries and Memoirs 1746–1843*. Stirling, 1942.

SIR ARCHIBALD GEIKIE, *Scottish Reminiscences*. Glasgow, 1908.

ELIZABETH GRANT OF ROTHIEMURCHUS, *Memoirs of a Highland Lady 1797–1827*, revised and edited by Angus Davidson. London, 1950.

HENRY HAMILTON, *An Economic History of Scotland in the Eighteenth Century*. Oxford, 1963.

SIR JOHN SINCLAIR, BART., *Statistical Account of Scotland Drawn up from the Communications of the Ministers of the Different Parishes*, 21 vols. Edinburgh, 1791–9.

Index

Index

Index